For Agnès

Spoilt Rotten

'Not since Christopher Hitchen's assault on Mother Theresa have so many sacred cows been slaughtered in such a slim volume.' *Spectator*

'Surgical demolition.' *Guardian*

'[A] cultural highlight.' *Observer*

'Outstanding…' Toby Young, *Mail on Sunday*

'Witty, always punchy.' *Scotsman*

'What make sentimentality so much worse.' *Sunday Telegraph*

'Entertaining.' *Express*

'Inimitable.' *Spectator*

'One of our most celebrated essayists.' *Mail on Sunday*

Litter

'What a book.' *Country Life*

'A little oasis of sanity and truth.' *Daily Mail*

'Very clever.' *Mail on Sunday*

'A rare voice of truth.' *Spectator*

'Pleasurable tartness.' *Guardian*

'Characteristically brilliant.' *Sunday Times*

The Knife Went In

'Nobody has observed the… fallacies of modern England with a clearer eye, or a more intelligent quill. It would be nice to know that the BBC had heard of him because we could expect to hear him deliver next year's Reith Lectures.' *Sunday Telegraph*

'A razor-sharp exposé of our broken society… Both funny and a badly needed corrective to conventional wisdom… hugely readable … gripping real-life stories… tells a deep truth about the sort of society we have become. A future historian, a century hence, will learn more about twenty-first-century Britain from this book than from any official document… Please read it.'
Peter Hitchens, *Mail on Sunday*

'Dalrymple is… [o]ne of the most interesting men of our times… There is nothing in his tale to celebrate, yet in the telling he deserves the commendation of anybody who values human civilisation.' *The Times*

'Lucid prose … an Orwellian dislike of cant, moral relativism and sloppy thinking… black humour.' *The Oldie*

'For anyone interested in the real world of ciminals and the criminal mind … the follies of the bureaucracy that envelops our penal system. The blackest of black humour… the best of humanity.' *Daily Mail*

THEODORE DALRYMPLE

In Praise of
Folly

THE BLIND-SPOTS
OF OUR MIND

THEODORE DALRYMPLE

London

GIBSON SQUARE

That is the land of lost content,
    I see it shining plain,
The happy highways where I went
    And cannot come again.

A.E. Housman, A Shropshire Lad

This edition published for the first time by Gibson Square in 2019.

Available as an e-book

    rights@gibsonsquare.com
    www.gibsonsquare.com
    Tel: +44 (0)20 7096 1100 (UK)
    Tel: +1 646 216 9813 (USA)

Contents

1

Everywhere is Interesting
'I've been to England'

On a trip to hard-living Dylan Thomas's hometown Laugharne in South-West Wales, I wanted to consider the folly of eminent people. My wife, who is also a psychiatrist, travelled with me from Bridgnorth, Shropshire, and Laugharne is on the estuary of the Tawe, Carmarthenshire. Dylan Thomas lived there at the idyllic Boathouse, perched on the river bank, for four years before his death. In another life, I would like to have been a bohemian myself and I always visit the pretty churchyard where he is buried. Serendipitously, the journey also passes by a number of second-hand bookshops, another obsession of mine.

My work has been, and still is, my greatest pleasure and there is no greater good fortune in life than this, perhaps. But it does mean that other kinds of enjoyment seem both unimportant to me and an interruption. We decided nonetheless to take a couple of days off and the fact that our roof had recently leaked and an old garden wall nearly collapsed may well have encouraged us. We chose the destination both for sentimental reasons and because we knew that there are few more beautiful drives in the country. Within a few hundred yards of our door, we are in the lovely Shropshire countryside; and the beauty continues with scarcely a break for a hundred and forty miles.

The sentimental reason for the trip was that we had already spent several months in Carmarthenshire. After her hospital consultancy, my wife spent a few months of each year occupying locum posts, and she had twice occupied them in Carmarthen. I always accompanied her and made what life I could wherever she went. I did not find this at all difficult, for the one lesson I have distilled from life is that everywhere is interesting. And South-West Wales is far from the least interesting place in the world.

Generally we stayed in hospital accommodation and sometimes it was dismal—in Yeovil, pronounced You-evil by the lady in our satnav, there were even bedbugs. But, though it was not of the standard of comfort or grace to which we had become accustomed, it was strangely liberating. In the first place, it took us back in time to when we were students and this in itself was pleasing. But in the second, it simplified life greatly by depriving us almost completely of household responsibilities. If something went wrong, there was someone on hand to fix it at no cost or irritation to ourselves. There was even someone to make our beds and clean our rooms. The kitchens were generally communal and we seldom availed ourselves of them, eating in restaurants instead. I, at any rate, felt free as a bird.

The first time my wife was employed in Carmarthen we stayed in the town itself, in a house on the grounds of the former mental hospital, now used for NHS administration after the original patients had moved out. But between her first and second period of employment in Carmarthen the house had been sold off and so we had to stay in hospital accommodation in Llanelli, a town of ill-repute.

Coal and steel towns are never pretty, but there is something peculiarly dispiriting about a steel town once the coal and steel have departed, as they now have from Llanelli. To the casual observer, the town's main economic activity of late seems to be the administration of unemployment and the recycling of government appropriations. In so far as there is any private economic activity at all, it is the expenditure of those subventions in the kind of chain stores that disfigure every British shopping district. Appearances, however, may be deceiving.

Dispiriting as Llanelli appeared to be at first sight, I was happy there (as, I think, I could be almost anywhere). I liked the people: they had more than the usual small-town warmth and friendliness. At bus-stops they would strike up a conversation with me as if it were the most natural thing to do, rather than an intrusion on privacy. They seemed interested in me, perhaps because not many strangers take buses in Llanelli. When they discovered that I was a doctor they asked my medical advice, which was flattering. To judge from overheard conversations, illness, doctors and hospitals were subjects of even greater interest to them than for most of mankind.

Three encounters of our time in Llanelli have stuck in my mind. At one of the bus stops I used to meet a man, a widower, in his middle seventies. He was going into town for his regular lunchtime pint of beer and he was always immaculately turned out for the event. He wore a blazer, grey trousers and highly-polished black shoes. His shirt was starched white, perfectly ironed, and he wore an elegant blue-and-red striped tie. He was splendid to behold, especially in the general sartorial slovenliness and bad taste that prevailed in Llanelli.

He had been a coal miner all his life, and his retirement coincided with the closure of the last coal mine. He seemed to have escaped entirely the occupational diseases of coal miners, and though to most of us the prospect of working down a pit all our life would be appalling, he had enjoyed his work and said he would not have done anything else.

His smartness of dress was not vanity but practical philosophy. Self-respect (he told me) required that he looked smart when he was in public. He dressed not for himself but for others, and it would be morally wrong to be an eyesore for them. It was therefore the reverse of egotism: rather, his attention to dress was a social virtue. It could not, as a widower, have been easy for him—I did not enquire what help, if any, he received.

On fine days—and in my memory there were many—I would go to my favourite place in the town, the churchyard of Holy Trinity, Felinfoel, and lie in the grass to read between the gravestones. Whatever we may think of the Victorians (Holy Trinity is a Victorian church), no one can deny that they were good at cemeteries. Their gravestones—pillars, angels, gothic arches, restrained and formal religious inscriptions—are infinitely more pastoral than our polished slabs that look like upright sections of the tops of kitchen islands, inscribed with carved golden lettering saying something like: *Goodnight, Dad.* The churchyard was a romantic place, deserted and perfectly peaceful, and generally it was poetry that I read there, before swiftly falling asleep.

One afternoon I woke from my sleep and to my surprise saw a middle-aged Punjabi woman dressed in *salwar kameez* nearby. She was carrying a bouquet of flowers. When she saw that I had woken she approached me and asked in imperfect English whether I knew where the grave of Margaret Davies was. Although I had in fact walked round the churchyard several times, reading the inscriptions, I had not committed the names to memory: and Margaret Davies, after all, was a common name hereabouts. I excused myself with the usual apology that I was not from here, but I offered to help her find it.

As we searched together, unsuccessfully in the event, I asked her why she sought for the grave. She told me that when she had first come to Britain, many years before, she had lived in Llanelli next door. Margaret Davies had been very nice to her. Since moving away from Llanelli she had heard that Margaret had died and was buried here. She wanted to put flowers on the grave in remembrance of her neighbour's kindness.

An even finer instance of integration followed soon afterwards. My wife and I ate in restaurants, but the choice in Llanelli was not large and we went frequently to an Indian restaurant—not because it was of exceptional quality, but because, like Mount Everest, it was there. Most of the time it was not well patronised, and we fell to talking to the waiter, a young man of Bangladeshi descent, but with a strong Welsh accent. We asked him in the course of one conversation whether he had ever been abroad.

'Yes,' he replied.

'Where?' we asked.

'I've been to Bangladesh,' he said.

'Anywhere else?'

'Yes, I've been to England.'

2

Natural Selection
The Staffordshire Bull Terrier

We set off at the appointed time—appointed by ourselves, that is. We have not mastered the art of travelling light and even a day trip seems often to end up more like moving house than a little jaunt. My wife envisages disaster *en route* and therefore takes clothes in case we are away for longer than planned. I take books enough to last a lifetime.

Our first destination was Ludlow, twenty miles from home, to have lunch with friends. They used to live in the tiny village of Stoke St Milborough, a few miles from Ludlow, in a lovely ancient cottage that approximated to everyone's dream of the English countryside. The path leading to the front door was through an avenue of old apple trees. On a fine day, it was impossible not to think there of Rupert Brooke: 'all evil shed away... dreams happy as her day... in hearts of peace, under an English heaven.'

Life is never like that, at least not for long. The garden in which the cottage sat was on a slope through which ran a babbling brook. Babbling, that is, until it roared after a downpour of rain and flooded the garden, which always required some kind of repair afterwards. Moreover, in hard winter weather the roads to the house became impassable. No doubt this would all be charmingly isolated for a young couple, to be recalled with nostalgia in later years how they were cut off in winter. But my friends were no longer young.

Earlier ages might have had their culture and cultivation, but we have cookery. One of the things about England whose passing I do not in the least regret is the food of my childhood and youth: the overcooked meat, the colour of the flesh of the corpse I dissected during my medical studies, and the vegetables seemingly boiled days in advance as if flavour were a bacterial poison to be neutralised by prolonged heat. Then there were the terrible things eaten as puddings that caused foreigners to exclaim, 'does one eat it or has it been eaten?' British cooks fought against flavour and triumphed turning meals into a regrettable necessity.

Since the age of spam and semolina, the population seems to have divided in two, gastronomically as much as economically. There are those, probably the more numerous, who subsist on fast food of meat-ish material fried in dubious oil and served with enigmatic sauces. And there are those who eat with discrimination so that many provincial towns and cities have excellent restaurants where once there was a culinary desert.

Ludlow is, for its size, probably the best town for restaurants in the country, if not the least spoilt. My friends chose a café open only for lunch. Being a simple place, the staff did not give you the impression that they were casting their pearls before swine. One of the attractions, apart from its food made entirely from local ingredients (the quince jelly was by far the best I have ever had), is that the café overlooks the banks of the River Teme, by a weir. The Teme is a salmon river and, in the season, returning salmon supposedly leap the weir to reach their spawning ground.

Deep inland as the town is, I found this not entirely easy to believe; but then, towards the end of our meal, I saw a salmon try (unsuccessfully) to clear the barrier. My first thought was that I had imagined it, that it was a figment of suggestion, for we had been talking shortly before of salmon and how a ladder had been built into the weir to make life easier for the fish. My friend said that someone had calculated that each salmon in the Teme cost the country £8000 to encourage, protect and preserve.

The episode brought back a memory of childhood. I saw a fox in our London garden when I was about nine or ten and rushed excitedly to my father to tell him what I had seen. He did not believe me; on the contrary, he thought I was being foolish or mendacious. But shortly afterwards there were reports of an invasion of foxes into urban areas, and now it is said that there are more urban foxes than rural ones. It taught me a good and a bad lesson—most lessons are both—confidence in my own judgment, and overconfidence in my own judgment.

The fleeting sight of the salmon leaping was to me both joyful and reassuring. Perhaps it was one of those consolatory intimations of immortality of which Wordsworth speaks:

What though the radiance which was once so bright
Be now for ever taken from my sight,
Though nothing can bring back the hour
Of splendour in the grass, of glory in the flower;
We will not grieve, rather find
Strength in what remains behind…

The life history of the salmon (and that of the eel) seems not merely remarkable to me, but astonishing and mysterious. Can the theory of natural selection by means of tiny increments of advantage in survival caused by random genetic mutation explain their convoluted life cycle?

It is not that I have any better explanation to propose but not having a better explanation is not enough to make the offered explanation true. On the one hand natural selection has always seemed to me circular. Some creatures survive better than others because they are fitter in their circumstances, their fitness being proved by the fact they are there. And the ease with which the theory explains almost any conduct of any creature, however different it is from that of a similar creature, seems to me not a strength but a weakness.

On the other hand, it is obvious that life on earth has changed and is changing, and that selective pressure can bring about rapid changes. As any book about the different breeds of dogs demonstrates, it is not only in their appearance but in their character that they vary. Selective pressure, in this case from dog owners, can bring about rapid differences in the populations of the breeds. A breed that was rarely seen until recently, the Staffordshire bull terrier, is now very common, at least in those areas of our town and cities where men (and increasingly women) want to look tough. Thus, animal selection tells us something about the direction of human society, too.

3

Shame
A Most Democratic Institution

Another source of consolation in Ludlow, apart from its beauty and the far-sighted decision of its council not to permit chain stores to set up in its main streets, is the presence of Mr Trevor Lloyd, bookbinder. Mr Lloyd has a workshop there of an old-fashioned type whose atmosphere conveys immediately craft of the very highest order, workmanship approaching the status of art. Everything is unhurried, attention to detail is meticulous, taste is impeccable, nothing is merely good enough. Mr Lloyd is famous in the little world of bibliophiles. He is spoken of with awe by other bookbinders, and I have heard him described on more than one occasion as the finest in Europe, if not the world.

On this occasion, I resisted the temptation to visit him. He had had a couple books of mine for more than a year, but 'genius,' said Carlyle, 'is an infinite capacity for taking pains.' It does not follow, of course, that an infinite capacity for taking pains is genius, but our world of mass convenience is not propitious to the exercise of that infinite capacity. In Bridgnorth market there is a man who has a stall of old tools, a hundred years old or more. These tools were certainly utilitarian but at the same time fashioned with an instinct for form, so that an ebony-and-brass spirit level, for example, is an object of enduring beauty. Whoever made it concentrated deeply on its form; whoever owned it treasured it. What is conveniently and immediately replaceable, on the other hand, is easily taken for granted.

Mr Lloyd, who was once a school teacher, has been a bookbinder for many years. If you take an unusual book to him he knows its history at once, not just the history of the contents but of the actual copy in hand, deduced from the slightest clues. I once took to him a copy of Henry Edwards Davis's *An Examination of the Fifteenth and Sixteenth Chapters of Mr Gibbon's History of the Decline and Fall of the Roman Empire, in Which His View of the Progress of the Christian Religion is Shewn to be Founded on the Misrepresentation of the Authors He Cites*, interleaved by a contemporary anonymous handwritten commentary favourable to Davis's aspersions on Gibbon's character and honesty, as well as a copy of Charles Bell's *A Dissertation on Gunshot Wounds*. The first was published in 1778 and the latter in 1814, but both had since undergone philistine rebinding. Davis had been rebound in shiny boards of shocking pink that could not have been altogether easy to find. As for the book by Bell, the re-binder had no respect for its physical quality, including the magnificent though melancholy drawings by the author (surgeon, anatomist, neurologist and artist, the first describer of the palsy that bears his name) of those wounded, fatally, by gunshot. When Mr Lloyd returned the books to me, they were once again in exquisite bindings appropriate to the year of publication.

The books he had of me latterly for restoration were a

splendid folio prayer book of 1693, and Jeremy Taylor's *XXV Sermons Preached at Golden-Grove: Being for the Winter Half-year, Beginning on Advent-Sunday, untill Whit-Sunday.* On seeing these books, Mr Lloyd, not unreasonably, asked me whether I was religious, or specially interested in religious books.

It is curious that it is more damaging socially these days to be thought religious than to be thought the opposite, and I found myself anxious to disavow any tendency to piety or religion. Pious is more likely nowadays to be used as a term of abuse than of praise, having the connotation of unctuous hypocrisy rather than of virtue. I am indeed still free (if that is the word) of religious belief, but I have no hostility to religion, at least not of the milder sort, and have no desire to rid anyone of what I think are their illusions; all the more so since I cannot claim to have a consistent or fully-formed philosophy of life myself. I no more know where the world came from or why there is something rather than nothing than that I can speak Amharic.

Moreover—and this has come as something of a surprise to me—I have developed a sympathy for the writings of the English divines, not only because of their movingly sonorous prose, but also for their often-generous sentiment. There is something consolatory in the words, even when you do not believe in the doctrine behind them. They seem somehow to go deeper and to call us to, whatever we may believe, reflect upon the limits of our own lives. Here is a passage chosen at random by letting the book fall open:

'The effect of this consideration [the suffering attendant on human existence] is this, that the sadnesses of this life help to sweeten the bitter cup of death. For let our life be never so long, if our strength were great as that of oxen or camels, if our sinews were strong as the cordage at the foot of an oak, if we were as fighting and prosperous people as *Siccius Dentatus* [a Roman tribune, fifth century BC], who was on the prevailing side in a hundred and twenty battles, who had three hundred and twelve public rewards assigned to him by his generals and princes for his valour and conduct in sieges and sharp encounters, and, besides all this, had his share in nine triumphs; yet still the period shall be that all this shall end in death, and the people shall talk of us awhile, good or bad, according as we deserve, or as they please, and once it shall come to pass that concerning every one of us it shall be told in the neighbourhood, that we are dead.'

Death, Taylor reminds, is the most democratic of institutions; and he reminds us also, in his *The Rules and Exercises of Holy Dying* (1651), from which I have just quoted, of our ineradicable frailty that should be sufficient to induce a degree of modesty in us, no matter how important we may think we are.

Golden Grove, where Taylor preached the sermons that Mr Lloyd was rebinding for me, was the country seat of Lord Carbery. It was the direction in which we were headed. Carbery alone of the Welsh aristocracy was dispossessed of his estate by Oliver Cromwell and Taylor was a royalist and spent much the Civil War and the subsequent Commonwealth in retreat at Golden Grove. The house, burned down and was completely destroyed in 1729. Could it be that Gerard Manley Hopkins's poem, 'Spring and Fall: to a Young Child', references the house that was once deemed of unsurpassed loveliness, but was no more?

Margaret, are you grieving
Over Goldengrove unleaving?
Leaves like the things of man, you
With your fresh thoughts care for, can you?

The poem is clearly about the painfully transitory nature of human existence and 'the things of man' such as houses like Golden Grove—though one commentary on 'Spring and Fall' speculated that its Goldengrove was an imaginary paradise.

There is no consolation in it, except the beauty of the poem itself. It was written in 1880, by which time Hopkins had spent four years in Wales, albeit in the North rather than the South-West, during which time he had gone to the trouble of learning Welsh well enough to write poetry in it.

Manley Hopkins was a man who, while still an Anglican before his conversion to Catholicism, would have read Taylor and learned about his life. A psychoanalyst, in addition to noting the Freudian slip, might see in the name chosen by Hopkins a symbol of his abandoned religion, Anglicanism—by then already deep in the throes of its melancholy, long, withdrawing roar; in the present time reduced to the merest sigh. There is another Golden Grove, an Elizabethan manor much altered in the reign of Queen Anne, and still standing, but in North Wales.

The Golden Grove of Lord Carbery was in the parish of Llanfihangel where Taylor also preached. The Welsh, a poetic nation, seem lacking in fertility when it comes to place names. There are many Llanfihangels (churches of St Michael) in Wales. Golden Grove was in Llanfihangel Aberbythych.

When my wife was working in Carmarthen we became interested in the extraordinary case of Sarah Jacob, the Welsh-Fasting Girl, who lived in the parish of Llanfihangel-ar-Arth a century and a half ago. A book by Sian Busby, *A Wonderful Little Girl*, had not long before been published to considerable acclaim. But the real expert on the case was Dr John Cule, a former psychiatrist and medical historian who wrote an excellent and scholarly, but largely and undeservedly forgotten, book, *Wreath on the Crown*, about the case, published in 1967. I discovered that Dr Cule was living in retirement in Capel Dewi, and when I contacted him he invited me to lunch.

He was then in his ninetieth year, living on his own in a cottage. He had prepared a simple but good meal and was dressed smartly in a tweed jacket and bow tie. When I saw him, I immediately resolved that at that time in my life, if I survived that long, I would not venture forth from my house except as well turned out.

Sarah Jacob was the daughter of Welsh-speaking farmers, by no means of the poorest class, though they spoke no English. In North Wales, my wife—a doctor specialising in psychogeriatrics—had sometimes to interview patients through an interpreter, for old people when confused often revert to their mother tongue. When my wife, who is French, mentions to people in France that her patients spoke Welsh, they invariably assume that Welsh is but a dialect of English and that she can understand it. They are astonished to learn that Welsh is more different from English than English from French.

Sarah was a girl of lively disposition, intelligent, religious, imaginative and romantically inclined. She was the third of seven children then living of Evan and Hannah Jacob, all of whom were well looked after. At the age of ten she developed an illness of an unspecified nature, which seems to have taken on a hysterical nature. From that time she was never normal again and took to her bed until her death at the age of twelve. In the last two years of her life she was said by her parents to have taken neither a morsel to eat nor a drop to drink, and many credulous people came to believe it, including the vicar of Llanfihangel-ar-Arth.

Since the girl, like everyone else in the area, was highly religious, this extraordinary situation was believed by them to be of supernatural or miraculous origin. Sarah Jacob's fame spread, and eventually she became the object of curiosity and even religious devotion for people from miles around, and even from as far away as Southampton. On visiting her, they left money on her breast. She was dressed in angelic garb, with a wreath of flowers on her pillow. The parents believed fully in the miraculous nature of the girl's fast, for she appeared healthy, plump and well fed despite it, and continued to grow; and as they slept in the same room as she they thought that they would have detected fraud, had there been any.

The case attracted attention throughout the country; a controversy raged as to precisely how long it was possible for humans to go without food and drink. In the end it was decided to send a bevy of professional nurses from Guy's Hospital down to Llanfihangel-ar-Arth to observe her closely, twenty-four hours a day, and to allow her no other visitors but her parents, who, of course, also fell under the observation of the nurses. The latter acted under the direction of doctors, who stipulated that under no circumstances should they give the 'Wonderful Little Girl', as she was then known, anything to drink or eat.

After a week of the regime of strict observation, Sarah Jacob was dead, not from starvation, as everyone in those days thought, but from dehydration. The nurses, under strict orders from the doctors, simply watched her die.

In effect, Sarah Jacob preferred death to exposure as a fraud. After her death, the nurses, doctors and her parents were charged with manslaughter, but the case against the doctors and nurses was soon dropped, leaving the parents alone to face the legal music. They were tried in Carmarthen and found guilty of manslaughter by gross neglect and sentenced to terms of imprisonment: twelve months in the father's case and six months in the mother's. The motive ascribed to them by the prosecution was, of course, monetary; for while their daughter maintained her fraud, of which it was alleged they must have been fully cognisant, considerable sums of money accrued to them. Their defence was that the money was given to Sarah, not themselves, but this, naturally, seemed pretty feeble. However, the fact is that for most of their daughter's alleged fasting period, until her story was publicised in the newspapers and became known through the countryside, they made no money at all from her.

In essence, they were convicted for their peasant ignorance and credulity. The nurses and even more the doctors who instructed the nurses, were surely the more culpable. And even at this distance of time, one feels the horrible injustice done by those in authority so anxious to exonerate their peers.

After lunch, Dr Cule took me to see the tomb of the Jacob family in the churchyard of Llanfihangel-ar-Arth. Standing at the tomb the tragic nature of the story seemed to come home to me more powerfully than before. First, we ourselves invest stones with an aura and then claim that the stones affect us by their aura. But if that is a fallacy, it is one from which we shall never liberate ourselves until all the famous houses that are open to the public receive no more visitors.

I noticed on the tomb that Evan and Hannah Jacob had a further child, a daughter, after they were released from prison having served their sentences. Dr Cule told me an interesting story regarding her.

When he started his research into the case in the late 1950s, this last child of the Jacobs' was still alive. But no one in the village told him so, although they knew it very well because she still lived there, and they knew that he was researching a book on the subject. Small Welsh villages were then, and to a large extent still are, mistrustful of strangers. Though he moved to Capel Dewi forty years ago and he was a Welsh-speaker, Dr Cule was still known there as 'the Incomer.' When he asked a villager when he would stop being called by that name, they replied, 'When the last man who remembers your arrival dies.'

Narrowness of horizon gives a strong individual flavour to a people; and for myself I often wish that I had such strong local roots, but without the narrowness that comes with them. In short, I want to be rooted and rootless at the same time, a typical example of the contradictory desires that the human heart finds room for.

Why did the villagers not tell him that the last daughter of the Jacobs was still alive? He thought that it was because they still felt ashamed that members of their community had been to jail and brought shame on it. In fact, they were reluctant to talk about the case at all. I thought of another possible explanation: shame not at the imprisonment of Evan and Hannah Jacob, but at the superstition and gullibility that the local people had displayed, who believed so strongly in the miraculous nature of Sarah Jacob's alleged fast.

In a near contemporary account, *A Complete History of the Case of the Welsh-Fasting Girl (Sarah Jacob) with Comments thereon and Observations on Death from Starvation*, by Thomas Fowler M.D., a local doctor, Dr Thomas Jones, is recorded as having written to the *Welsh Observer* at the height of the mania: 'The time will come... when this miracle will be a shame and a stench in the whole country... synonymous with disgrace.' So it proved. Tiny, closed communities have long historical memories, completely at variance with what might be called the presentism, the forgetful immersion in the affairs of the present, of more modern societies.

Dr Cule took me to the farmhouse where the dramatic events of 1867 to 1869 took place. We passed the pub where the coroner's inquest after her death had been held—coroner's inquests and even post mortems in those days were often held in pubs—and then drove down a track to the house called Llethernyadd-Ucha. It was now attached to a working farm, and in a somewhat dilapidated state, being used to store farm implements and machines. Dr Cule had called the owners beforehand, who kindly gave us permission to come on to their land. But they were a little mystified by our wish to do so. There was nothing in or on or about the house, whose thatch had been replaced by tin, to commemorate the historic events (as I now thought of them) that had taken place.

This was a powerful reminder that my strange serial obsession (I still read anything on the case that I can find) is peculiar to me and perhaps to a small number of other people.

4

Pain in the Room
Shocking Pink

There used to be a second-hand bookshop in Ludlow, but there is no longer. It was there that, a number of years before, I had bought the shocking-pink-covered refutation of Gibbon's famous fifteenth and sixteenth chapters, the chapters in which he explained the rise of Christianity not by the workings of divine providence, but by operation of secular causes—not all of them flattering to the religious point of view. Second-hand bookshops can barely survive, however, in fashionable towns such as Ludlow. The rents are too high, and the general public, which has an infinite appetite for ornaments, alternative medicine and health-food products, has none at all for musty old books.

Nonetheless, there still is an antiquarian bookseller in Ludlow. By coincidence I had bought a book from him through the internet shortly before, and the friends whom we were visiting were friends of his. I had never met him and, Ludlow being small, he was but a short walk away. His business was entirely online, but he welcomed visitors such as I, whose main discretionary expenditure was on books.

He lived in a beautiful eighteenth-century house, wonderfully furnished. We discussed briefly the state of the trade—very bad and getting worse. The problem was that the last generation to be interested in old books was thinning out and was not being replaced by young people from a generation increasingly obsessed by electronic gadgetry and who regarded a page on a screen as a long text. Like Talleyrand before the French Revolution, we felt that no one who had not known the pleasures of the browse through antiquarian book shelves had known the full sweetness of life. Though I did not like to interrupt our nostalgia, the strange thing was that the price of old books was not falling. If fewer people were interested in them, surely their price should fall? This paradox, he pinned to the fact that the older book-loving generation may have reduced in size, but its economic power had increased compared to the young.

We went down into his capacious cellar where his books were ranged. He showed me a first edition in English, in pristine condition, of Newton's *Principia*, with the title *The Mathematical Principles of Natural Philosophy*, a marvellous book for those alive not only to its content (the greatest intellectual advance, said Einstein, that it has ever been given to one man to make) but to the physical beauty of early eighteenth century scientific illustration and diagrams. I hardly dared hold it for, not having been raised in the midst of precious objects, I have a habit of dropping or otherwise damaging the most valuable things out of sheer nervousness; besides which I did not want to give the impression that I might possibly buy such a book.

Left alone among the shelves, I was as happy as a bookworm. I can spend hours reading the first paragraphs of a thousand books, no matter how recondite their subject matter. I even relish books with titles such as *A Brief*

History of Banking in Plaistow or *The Influence of Calvinism on Trade Unionism in Aberdeen*. The real bookworm, *trogium pulsatorium*, must be under evolutionary threat, for its once ubiquitous habitat—mouldy, dark, dusty, dank, and neglected shelves, filled with old books whose paper has not been treated chemically has all but disappeared. When I find an old book with the neat little holes sometimes running through hundreds of pages made by bookworms—pinholed, as the booksellers say—I am filled with admiration for nature's infinite devices.

Among the cheaper volumes was a biography of Stephen Hales, D.D., F.R.S., by A.E. Clark-Kennedy, published in 1929. Both subject and author were men of great stature—in Clark-Kennedy's case physical as well as intellectual and moral—and this particular copy of his biography had an interesting biography of its own.

The reverend Stephen Hales was one of those many Church-of-England clergymen who saw in the regularities of the physical world proof of divine providence. By investigating those regularities with painstaking experimentation such clergymen thought that they were performing a religious duty. There are still scientists who believe that uncovering the intricacies of the universe can only increase admiration for, divine wisdom. While there is a great deal of what used, in the eighteenth century, to be called 'natural evil' in the world, such as earthquakes, hurricanes and horrible parasitism, occasionally, most often following the first glass of wine after a busy day, I almost share in these clergymen's oceanic feelings of universal wellbeing. All is right with the world, even if it's wrong, in the words of Alexander Pope in *An Essay on Man*, 1734:

> Safe in the hand of one disposing Pow'r,
> Or in the natal, or the mortal hour.
> All Nature is but Art, unknown to thee;
> All chance, direction, which thou canst not see;
> All discord, harmony not understood;
> All partial evil, universal good:
> And, spite of pride, in erring reason's spite,
> One truth is clear, whatever is, is right.

The reverend Hales was a great scientist with a wide range of interests and a long list of achievements. In those days science could still be done in rectories and he discovered a great deal about the physiology of plants. But from a doctor's point of view his experiments on the ventilation of ships and prisons in order to reduce gaol fever, and on the circulation of the blood, are what lend him immortality. It was natural for people, including Hales, to have supposed that the epidemics of typhus that killed so many prisoners and sailors arose from the stale and foetid air they breathed in the overcrowded and ill-ventilated spaces in which they were kept. On the assumption that the disease was spread by the air, Hales invented a system of ventilation of Newgate Prison that seemed to reduce the death rate from 'gaol fever' very considerably. According to Hales:

'In the year 1749, of 200 men but one died, and he of the small-pox. And in the year 1750, of 240 who were there three months, but two died. In the year 1751, none died;

And, in the year 1752, only one old person died. Whereas, before the ventilators were put up, there often died 50 or 100 of the infectious gaol-distemper.'

In actual fact, typhus is spread by body lice. There were many instances where prisoners spread the disease to the judges in court, whose robes, presumably, were splendidly adapted to harbour lice, and who subsequently died of the same disease as the accused whom they were trying. It is difficult to imagine, the cause of gaol fever being what it was, how Hales's ventilators could have done much to prevent its spread. Freshening the air, however desirable in itself, would not have reduced the number of body lice harboured by the inmates, which is a consequence of dirt and overcrowding. If Hales's figures for the deaths in Newgate are accurate, he provides a better explanation for the reduced mortality in the subsequent lines:

'And what contributes the more to the present healthiness of the place, is that Mr Hayward, the Master of the Prison, continues with the same care and zeal to keep it clean.'

Hales is best-known for having been the first man to have measured blood pressure. He did so to refute the prevalent theory of the time that blood was propelled round the body by the contraction of the muscles through which the blood ran. He wanted to demonstrate that it was propelled instead by the force of the contraction of the heart. The description of his experiment to prove it, published in his book *Haemastaticks*, is alarming:

'I laid a common field gate on the ground, with some straw upon it, on which a white mare was cast on her right side, and in that posture bound fast to the gate.... Then laying open the left jugular vein, I fixed to that part of it which comes from the head, a glass tube, which was four feet and 2 inches long. The blood rose in it, in 3 or 4 seconds of time about a foot, and then was stationary for 2 or 3 seconds; then in 3 or 4 seconds more, it rose sometimes gradually, and sometimes with an unequally accelerated motion, 9 inches or more, on small strainings of the mare: then upon greater strainings.'

Hales realised that there was a possible objection to his experiment, namely that 'a considerable stream of blood was for a time stopped' by the blood in the tubes he had affixed to the mare's arteries and veins. To meet what he called this 'inconvenience,' he says:

'I fixed tubes laterally to the jugular veins and arteries of dog no 13... having laid the vein or artery bare, I drew a linen cloth under it, to wipe it very dry; and then placed under it one of the above-mentioned slit pieces of wood, laying the vein or artery in its cavity, which was covered with pitch, that was at that instant afresh melted with a small warm iron rod; then pouring the pitch, not very hot, over the vein or artery, I immediately put on the other half of the split wood, which had the hole bored thro' it, and tied them fast together: then entering the slender point of a knife into the above-mentioned hole.'

Hales discovered many things about blood pressure and the circulation, for example that the pressure was higher the larger the animal, and much lower in veins than in arteries; he discovered that the speed of the pulse is inversely proportionate to the size of the animal; that the

blood pressure was at its maximum during systole
(contraction of the heart's largest chambers); that blood
loss reduces the blood pressure, and increases the rate of
the pulse to compensate; and in general that the state of
the circulation depended on many factors, including
warmth, movement and excitement. He was the first to
have suggested that the change from dark purplish blood
to bright red blood that takes place in the lungs was caused
by something that the blood absorbed from the air.

Much of what he discovered now seems so obvious to
any first-year medical student that they will not readily
appreciate that it ever had to be discovered from a position
of complete ignorance, and that it was not remotely innate
human knowledge such as chimpanzees seem to have of
the dangerousness of snakes. Hales's experiments were
intellectually ingenious, practically difficult, and (for us)
horrible to read about, especially when you consider that
his account was a highly selective one from the whole of
his experiments.

Was Hales actuated by the desire to do good to
humanity or by scientific curiosity alone, or even by a thirst
for scientific glory? Did he think, for example, that the
truth about physiology would eventually set us free from
the scourge of illness, as truth in St John's gospel is said to
free us from the bondage of sin? Did he foresee that his
discovery that blood loss increased the pulse rate would
one day become a cardinal sign in medicine, or did he
simply find it an elegant contrivance that illustrated God's
infinite ingenuity?

Clark-Kennedy (himself the son of a clergyman) does

not say. There was no anaesthesia at the time, no way of lessening the animals' terror at being tied down and cut open. And the 'straining' to which Hales refers in his experiments must surely have been the animals attempts to escape their tormentor. The fact that he mentioned, in the first passage quoted above, that the mare was to be killed in any case because she had become what practitioners of mass euthanasia in Nazi Germany called 'a useless eater,' suggested, however, that Hales had an uneasy conscience, or at least was aware that readers might flinch when reading about the cruelty afflicted on the mare.

The reverend Hales leaves out much that might alarm the reader. 'Dog no 13'? How many more animals were sacrificed for his lust for knowledge? His experiments were most unlikely to have produced good results the first time round and he must have tried many techniques that did not work. Even in Hales's day, men loved their dogs, and would have quailed to think of such things done to their beloved canine. Although extreme forms of militancy on behalf of the supposed rights of animals were not known when Clark-Kennedy wrote his biography (though he lived into that era, dying aged ninety two in 1985), the anti-vivisectionist movement and that for the protection of animals was strong enough in 1929 for him to feel concern about the impression his account of Hales's experiment might have on his readership. His manner of dealing with possible ethical objections is unlikely to have reassured them:

'The reader, who, at first sight, feels inclined to criticise Hales's work on the grounds of cruelty, must remember that Bacon had recommended vivisection as a scientific method, and the discovery, partly through this means, of the circulation of the blood had brought it into prominence…. At that time even operations on man had to be performed without anaesthesia; the standards of unavoidable pain and suffering were naturally rather different then from those existing now. His experiments were performed to advance science, but it is important to remember that in those days cruelty to animals for quite useless purposes was general; bull-baiting was patronised by the aristocracy, bear-baiting and the brutal sport of cock-throwing were popular amusements among the lower classes.'

Why choose Francis Bacon as an authority on this subject? I know of no better example of begging the question. Dragging the discovery of the circulation of the blood into it implies not only that this knowledge could not have been obtained by any other method, but that the end, knowledge, justified the means, vivisection. As for the discovery's 'bringing into prominence' vivisection as a method, this is also question-begging: for it assumes that what has been done before justifies what we do now. And there surely is a considerable moral difference between an un-anaesthetised operation on a willing subject to remove, say, a cancer that threatens his life, and the suffering forced upon an animal to no possible benefit to itself. And it is at least questionable whether the amusement of crowds is 'a quite useless purpose,' given that the desire for amusement is perpetual among humans. But we do not believe that because something is generally done it is right to do it, even if someone benefits from it being done (as is almost always the case).

Nor was this the belief even in Hales's time. Clark-Kennedy himself points out that Alexander Pope who wrote 'whatever is, is right' in *An Essay on Man*, Hales's friend and neighbour while the latter was rector of Teddington, thought vivisection was profoundly wrong, regardless of what Bacon had said or the crowds drawn by bear-baiting. 'He commits most of these barbarities with the thought of being of use to man,' said Pope. 'But how do we know that we have a right to kill creatures that we are so little above as dogs, for our curiosity?'

Clark-Kennedy also quotes a satirical poem called 'The Boat' by the reverend George Twining, about a boat trip up the Thames:

> Green Teddington's serene retreat
> For Philosophic studies meet,
> Where the good Pastor Stephen Hales
> Weighed moisture in a pair of scales,
> To lingering death put Mares and Dogs,
> And stripped the skins of living Frogs.
> Nature, he loved, her Works intent
> To search or sometimes to torment.

While Hales was still alive, twenty-five years after he published the great book in which he announced so many discoveries, Doctor Johnson, in the *Idler* for August 8, 1758, published a furious attack on vivisection. Doctor Johnson was no obscurantist when it came to medicine. He wrote short biographies of two of the most important medical figures of the age, Thomas Sydenham and Herman Boerhaave, and was a firm believer in the power of medical science. He read the medical literature of his time and even dabbled in experiments himself. He had probably read Hales, for he lived in the last age in which a man could take an intelligent interest in most fields of human learning. As a man of many illnesses, moreover, he had good reason to interest himself in medicine.

Johnson starts with an almost Swiftian mockery of those who investigate nature by means of experiment, either finding nothing or what is perfectly obvious and already known:

'[T]he inferior professors of medical knowledge... whose lives are only varied by varieties of cruelty; whose favourite amusement is to nail dogs to tables and open them alive; to try how long life may be continued in various degrees of mutilation, or with the excision or laceration of the vital parts... and whether the more lasting agonies are produced by poison forced into the mouth, or injected into the veins.'

Johnson apologises for bringing these things to the attention of his readers, continuing that if they did not exist it would be best not to put them into anyone's mind, implying that knowledge of horrors is apt to increase their practice, an argument for restraint in the products of the imagination. The practice of cruelty or callousness in one sphere, says Johnson, leads to its practice in another:

'[T]he anatomical novice tears out the living bowels of an animal, and styles himself physician, prepares himself by familiar cruelty for that profession which he is to exercise upon the tender and the helpless, upon feeble bodies and broken minds, and by which he has opportunities to extend his arts of torture, and continue those experiments upon infancy and age, which he has hitherto tried upon cats and dogs.'

No doctor, at least no doctor who trained before virtual reality supplanted reality itself in the teaching and learning of physiology, will read these words of Doctor Johnson's without them provoking some examination of his conscience. For they, too, tortured animals in the physiology classes of their youth, supposedly to prove for themselves physiological laws that were already known and taught, and which his experiments, being those of a novice, would only imperfectly confirm. Even where the young researcher does an original experiment on living animals, as I myself once did, he is unlikely to extend knowledge by very much, if at all; and he hardens his heart to the creatures whom he 'sacrifices,' the word commonly used, to examine post mortem the effect of something or other done to them.

Doctor Johnson also writes:

'I know not, that by living dissections any discovery has been made by which a single malady is more easily cured. And if the knowledge of physiology has been somewhat increased, he surely buys knowledge dear, who learns the use of the lacteals at the expense of his humanity.'

Johnson was right at the time at which he wrote. It was to be nearly two centuries after the publication of *Haemastaticks* before Hales's discoveries were to be of any practical value to the ill or injured. The suffering of the animals on which he experimented was certain but the benefit to humanity of those experiments speculative and still only a matter of faith.

In a recent edition of the *British Medical Journal* (May, 2014) an article by a sociologist and an epidemiologist questioned the value of animal experimentation, at least as it is actually carried out, a view that was largely endorsed in an editorial by the editor. The authors brought two main charges against the experiments: the first was that the vast majority of them were so poorly conducted that they added little or nothing to our knowledge; and the second was that, because of differences of physiology and bio-chemistry, experiments on animals are often not applicable to humans.[1] The editor stated in his article: 'Even if the research were conducted faultlessly... our ability to predict human responses from animal models will be limited by interspecies differences in molecular and metabolic pathways.'

Or, more plainly, man is not a rat. No one doubted that, if its utility to humans were proved, there would be nothing left to say against animal experimentation. Nor did anyone deny that even with the use of anaesthetics animal experimentation caused suffering.

However, most scientists do not consider it a serious moral problem, at least where the experiments are interesting scientifically. For example, when I mentioned the question to a medical friend he cited a lecture given by an eminent researcher on the physiology of obesity before a select audience. The research he had conducted proved that there was a biochemical substance in fat mice that can induce obesity in thin mice. This was an important finding that has been found applicable to man, and might one day lead to a treatment for or prevention of obesity. He joined a fat and thin mouse together surgically, the thin mouse becoming fat under the conditions in which it had previously remained thin. No one in the audience protested that this was cruel, albeit physiologically informative.

What are the sufferings of mice compared with those of the obese? That is why (or rather one of the reasons why) Mrs Gradgrind's reply to the question whether she was in pain, 'I think there's a pain somewhere in the room, but I couldn't positively say that I have got it,' is so wonderfully funny.

Was the two-hundred-year gap between reverend Stephen Hales's horrific experiments and the useful application of his findings too long to justify them? The utilitarian belief that the infliction of suffering on animals is justified if there is 'a prospect of preponderant good'—in the words of Jeremy Bentham—attempts to provide a criterion. But this measure is not very useful if there is no way of knowing; whether or not any good will result, how close the connection has to be, how remote it can be, or what the size of the benefit compared with the suffering should be.

Dr Hales himself in the end—he was a clergyman after all—had doubts about the moral propriety of the suffering he caused, and Clark-Kennedy says that this might have been why, after he had published *Haemastaticks*, he never experimented again on sentient beings. His biographer says that there exists a letter in which he expressed his guilt. He devoted himself thenceforth to plant physiology, the ventilation of ships and prisons, and writing against the evils of gin.

Shortly after I read the biography I travelled on a bus from Bridgnorth to Wolverhampton, which was full of children who attended the grammar school there. One of the girls read her school essay on the ethics of vivisection to another sitting next to her on the bus. I did not catch all she read, but what I did catch was better-informed than I should have managed at her age: 'animals are often better experimental subjects than humans because of their shorter life-span... Man shares ninety-eight per cent of his genome with mice, which suffer from many of the same diseases as man... The removal the pancreas from dogs led directly to the discovery of insulin and the treatment of diabetes.'

1   There was excellent illustration of this in a recent paper in the *New England Journal of Medicine* (December 13, 2014), which reported a trial of progesterone, a steroid naturally occurring in females, in the treatment of severe traumatic brain injury. Why should such a trial be conducted, on what rationale? The introduction to the paper says 'Progesterone has been shown to have broad neuroprotective properties in multiple animal species and in a variety of models of neurologic injury... A total of 20 research groups working with four species and 22 different models have found neuroprotective effects of progesterone in more than 180 experimental pharmacologic studies.' The trial proved a complete failure: progesterone neither saved life nor improved outcome in humans suffering from Traumatic Brain Injury (TBI). The paper explained that 'Limitations in the ability to translate experimental data to the context of TBI in humans may also have contributed to the trial failures.' It delicately passed over the means by which head injuries were produced in 4 species in 22 different ways in 180 studies, mentioning neither the species involved nor the numbers sacrificed to this so far useless line of research.

5

Bullying
Guinea Pigs

My copy of Stephen Hales's biography once belonged to W.D.M. Paton, later Sir William Paton, who was professor of pharmacology at Oxford and one of the great pharmacologists of his time. He bought, or read, it in 1938, while he was still a student. While I am no great believer in graphology as a science, nevertheless, his hand, tending to the micrographic, is obviously that of a very neat and precise man. I happened later to find and buy a copy of a book by him, *Man and Mouse*, that was published forty six years later. It was his own copy, sent to him by his editor at the Oxford University Press, Nicola Bion, daughter of the well-known psychoanalyst Wilfred Bion. 'W.D.M.P.', says his inscription, 'From Nicola Bion 11 July 1984'. What is striking is that Sir William's hand is exactly the same as it was almost five decades years earlier.

This stability is interesting. If handwriting is, or at any rate can be, a reflection of our character, it suggests that our character is formed early in life—Paton was twenty one in 1938. By the time we die, few of the molecules with which we were born will subsist: and yet our handwriting, formed by the end of adolescence, will. I hesitate to call this a miracle, since it is commonplace, and yet it seems curious.

Did reading the biography of Hales influence Paton, scientifically and morally? Like Hales, he was a successful experimenter in more than one field. He nearly became a respiratory physiologist. Among his first work was an investigation into the physiology of divers and submariners and, as with everything he ever experimented on, he made important discoveries.

His first major pharmacological discovery was the release of histamine from cells of the body as the cause of reactions to certain drugs, another fact now so well-known among doctors that one forgets it ever had to be discovered. He went on to identify neuromuscular blocking agents of great use in surgery that were also the first drugs of value in the treatment of malignant hypertension, a form of high blood pressure that was until then uniformly (and quickly) fatal. He performed experiments on the physiology of addiction to opiate drugs, using the *ileum* (part of the small intestine) of guinea pigs as a model. He was the first academic pharmacologist to take an interest in cannabis, whose alleged harmlessness he long doubted. As with Hales, scientific curiosity was the main motive of Paton's research, though he also strongly believed that dis-interested science would benefit us in practical ways.

Paton (presumably as a young man) recorded in pencil on the front pastedown of Hales biography:

'There are two things in his character, which particularly distinguish him from almost every other man: the first was, that his mind was so habitually bent on acquiring knowledge, that, having what he thought an abundant income, he was solicitous to avoid any further preferment in the church, lest his time and attention might thereby be diverted from his other favourite and useful occupations. The other feature of his character was no less singular: he could look even upon wicked men, and those who did him unkind offices, without any emotion of particular indignation; not from want of discernment or sensibility; but he used to consider them only like those experiments which, upon trial, he found could never be applied to any useful purpose, and which he calmly and dispassionately put aside.'

The *Dictionary of National Biography* says of Paton's own character: 'At a personal level Paton was a calm and thoughtful individual, who seldom showed anger or strong emotion, except when confronted by uninformed prejudice, which he detested.'

A second page noted by Paton at the front was that on which the name of Dr John Addenbrooke appeared. Addenbrooke died in 1719, still a young man with no particular scientific achievements yet to his name, but he left a legacy of £4000 to found the hospital in Cambridge that still bears his name—his trustees taking their time, it was not founded until forty seven years after his death. Paton, who had no children, left money to charitable causes, too, in the field of pharmacology.

In an autobiographical paper published in 1986 in the *Annual Review of Pharmacology and Toxicology*, Paton addresses his predecessors. He mentions Hales in a list of scientists with whom he believes himself to be in apostolic succession:

'Soon after I had qualified in 1942, I saw an advertisement by an anti-vivisectionist society on a hoarding near our flat in London. It claimed to give the number of children dying from diphtheria over a term of ten years, who had been vaccinated against the disease. None of the relevant figures, about numbers at risk and the fate of the unvaccinated, were given. It stuck in my mind. Perhaps it prepared me for joint work... as chairman of the British Research Defence Society... how could anyone who had seen what medicine can do as a result of animal experimentation, who then sees that work traduced, fail to defend it?'

He includes a family anecdote of the bullying that it could lead to:

'I am very proud of my grandfather. David Macdonald was a Presbyterian minister in Derby in 1901, when Stephen Coleridge, the leading anti-vivisectionist of his day, came to lecture on animal experimentation. My grandfather, who was interested in science and bought *Nature* every week to circulate round his parish, did not like the style of what he heard. He criticised it vigorously at the meeting, citing Ferrier, Keith, and Spencer Wells, and then wrote to the local paper referring to 'suppressio veri' and 'suggestio falsi' and saying that no lover of truth could support Mr Coleridge's society. Coleridge then launched a suit for libel, demanding a public apology, damages and costs. Although David Macdonald was a poor man, he refused these. He had always been friendly with the local doctors, and in due course they came to his rescue, bringing in Lauder Brunton and Victor Horsley.[1] When the case came up, David Macdonald needed to do no more than show that there had been no personal attack; after 30 minutes, the jury asked if they needed to hear any more, returned a not-guilty verdict and said the case should never have been brought. It remains an exceptional case to my knowledge, of a member of the church putting himself at risk for the world of science.'

I myself am inclined to believe both the vivisectionists and the anti-vivisectionists: that the practice has contributed to knowledge that ultimately was of great benefit to both man and animals, but also that a considerable amount of useless suffering has been inflicted upon animals. These two are complimentary and not contradictory beliefs.

[1]   Sir Thomas Lauder Brunton (1844-1916) established the first laboratory in Britain devoted specifically to pharmacology and he was the first to establish the use of amyl nitrite for the relief of angina. Sir Victor Horsley (1857-1916) was a physiologist and surgeon, generally regarded as the founder of modern neurosurgery.

6

Heredity
Twisting Round a Stick

Some anti-vivisectionists at least have not been humanitarians. George Bernard Shaw who, like Tolstoy, was not only ignorant but militantly ignorant of medical matters, was a firm anti-vivisectionist, though he had no scruple at all about, indeed advocated, the killing of the old, infirm and unproductive. He always preferred a striking phrase to the most elementary truth. Among his aphorisms are the following:

> The vivisector is distinguished from the ordinary run of limited scoundrels by being an infinite scoundrel. The proper place in organised human society for a scoundrel who is prepared to seek knowledge or anything else without conscience is the lethal chamber.[1]

That tenderness of feeling towards animals is not always incompatible with murderous rage towards humans was proved to me by a patient dressed in military fatigues, who was so outraged by the way in which animals were farmed that he wanted to kill all the women at the meat-counter of his local supermarket, and to this end had joined a gun club. The Nazis had a strong anti-vivisectionist strain too (as Shaw had a strong Nazi-strain). There is a cartoon of Goering receiving the Nazi salute from all the guinea pigs and rabbits liberated by the Nazis from experimental laboratories. He is shown as the leader of the laboratory animals. This was not satire against, but rather was propaganda for the Nazis, to demonstrate the strength of their humanity.

Stephen Coleridge, the leader of the anti-vivisectionists at the end of the nineteenth and in the first two decades of the twentieth century, was not a negligible man. The great-great-nephew of Samuel Taylor Coleridge and son of the lord chief justice, Lord Coleridge, he was also the founder of the National Society for the Prevention of Cruelty to Animals. He was, in addition, instrumental in the agitation that prevented the establishment in Britain of a Pasteur Institute—though the British Institute of Preventive Medicine (now called the Lister Institute) was established in its place in 1891 as Britain's first medical-research charity. His book, *Vivisection: A Heartless Science*, was published in 1916, an odd year, perhaps, to protest at book-length against cruel practices against animals, when battles were taking place that inspired lines such as Wilfred Owen's: 'What passing-bells for these who die as cattle?'

But, as Bernard Shaw argued (in this case correctly), it is no defence against a charge of wrongdoing that you can find a much greater case of wrongdoing. By the time his book was published, Coleridge had been campaigning against vivisection for three decades. It would be a sorry world if no one ever attended to anything but that which was ethically most important.

As Paton was hereditarily pro-vivisection, Coleridge tells us that he was hereditarily against it, raising the question of how far we hold our opinions by descent. His father, the lord chief justice, was opposed to vivisection, as was his grandfather, the judge Sir John Coleridge. And Stephen interprets the concluding stanzas of his great-great uncle's 'The Rime of the Ancient Mariner' as having been anti-vivisectionist:

He prayeth best, who loveth best
All things both great and small;
For the dear God that loveth us,
He made and loveth all.

No one, however, can take this last line literally as an injunction. There is a website that satirises the incontinent reverence for all forms of life through its devotion to a spoof campaign to save the Guinea worm, *dracunculus medinensis*, from total eradication. The female adult of this revolting creature is a worm up to two feet long (the male being smaller, dying after copulation and being absorbed as a nutrient by the female). The female migrates to the outer edge of the foot of her human host, from which she extrudes her larvae into water when the foot is immersed. These are then ingested by water-fleas, which are in turn ingested by man in unclean water, and the whole distasteful cycle starts again. The adult worm, which in any leg may be multiple, can cause a variety of disabling systemic symptoms before it causes a break in the skin to extrude offspring, the traditional method of treatment being to wind it gradually around a stick, twisting a little more of it each day until it is entirely removed, taking care not to break it lest, by doing so, it causes abscess formation in the leg. Having been myself parasitised on by three of the less dangerous but nonetheless aesthetically unpleasing and inconvenient multicellular parasites of man, namely *tunga penetrans* (jiggers), *cordylobia anthropophaga* (tumbu fly) and *sarcoptes scabiei* (scabies, contracted from a patient with the most severe form of the infection, known as Norwegian), I do not wholly share the uncritical reverence for all forms of life—many, but by no means all.

Stephen Coleridge's greatest opponent was another Stephen, Stephen Paget, who was secretary of the Research Defence Society, set up to counteract the influence and propaganda of the anti-vivisectionists. He was yet another example of opinion by descent, for his father was the prominent surgeon, Sir James Paget, after whom Paget's diseases of the bone and of the nipple were named. It is the ambition of every doctor to achieve a strange kind of immortality by having a disease named after them because they were the first to describe or delineate it. Though these days there is something of a reaction against this practice, first because it is often found that the supposed first description of a disease was not truly the first, and second because the discoverer or describer is subsequently found to have been reprehensible.

Sir James, who as a lecturer in physiology and a firm believer in the value of vivisection, was also the first to realise (in 1849, while he was still very junior) that a certain grittiness of the muscle post mortem was actually caused by one of those other multicellular organisms that do not inspire automatic reverence for life: *trichinella spiralis*, the nematode worm that causes measly pork, one of the reasons why each carcass of pork has to be inspected and why eating undercooked pork is not a good idea. The life cycle of this creature is not attractive. The worm inhabits the rat, the rat is eaten by the pig, and the pig by man (bear meat will also spread trichinosis, but I have eaten very thoroughly cooked bear only once, in Romania). If the meat be undercooked, the larvae enter our striated muscles, or occasionally the heart or brain. Trichinosis can be anything from symptomless to fatal, though usually tending to the former.

I mention all this because my one attempt at experimental research happened to have been on the immunology of trichinosis in the guinea pig, which inoffensive creature the worm will also infect if fed to it. I was attempting to show—by means of isolated guinea-pig *ileum* taken after the guinea pig had been fed with the worm down a tube passed into the stomach and then 'sacrificed' a couple of weeks later—that the allergic reaction of guinea pig *ileum* to *trichinella* antigens was mediated by an as yet undiscovered chemical in the small intestines. What I discovered was equivocal at best and a lot of guinea pigs died so that I could prove nothing much.

Of course, I might have discovered something, and that something might have been important New things do not readily present themselves with the experiment being a matter of red tape. Unless you take the view, as Coleridge did not, that no knowledge bought at the expense of any live creature is or ever could be justified, analogous to pacifists, my experiment was warranted. As for the suffering of the guinea pigs, it is difficult to assess its magnitude. No doubt it was mildly unpleasant for them to be fed down a tube (the smell of the *trichinella* solution was unpleasant to the human nose), but the discomfort was transient. The experiment required that they were killed by violence, for a death by anaesthesia might have interfered with the physiology of their gut. It was intended to be quick and merciful, but it was not invariably successful in the way intended.

Stephen Paget, the secretary of the Research Defence Society, was an interesting character. He followed his father into the surgical profession, but never achieved his eminence or even a very large practice. He was notable for one surgical achievement (or concept), however. He was among the first to wonder why it was that different cancers metastasised in predictably different ways. He put forward the idea that there must be factors both in the tumour and the tissue to which it spread preferentially that explain the pattern: the seed and the soil, as he put it. This was reasoning from known facts rather than new experiments, however.

In his *Confessio Medici*, published anonymously in 1908, Paget describes how difficult it was to follow an eminent father into his profession, how inadequate the comparison made him feel, and how, in fact, he had never even matched the passion for the profession to the exclusion of all else that his father evidently had. He entered the medical profession, in effect, as many men did, from the mere need to do something with their lives. Despite his relatively easy path in early life by comparison with the one his father had been obliged to follow, in reality—in psychological reality, that is—his was far more difficult. One might therefore interpret his decision to become a full-time campaigner in defence of research on animals, rather than be a researcher himself, or even a practising surgeon, as a way of finding a purpose that allowed him to abandon his competition with his father without having either to abjure his influence altogether or to admit total defeat. He achieved eminence for himself in the end by a subtly parallel route.

To return to the other Stephen, in his *Vivisection*, Coleridge tells the following anecdote:

'At the time the cries and howls of the dogs at the laboratory of University College in Gower Street were reported to me by the neighbouring residents as being pitiful and distressing in the extreme. I therefore went to a house there and heard for myself the miserable clamour. Urged by a compelling desire to see what was going on I penetrated to the staircase, at the head of which was the door to the laboratory, and by the hand of the janitor proffered my card with a request to be shown its interior.

'I timed the disappearance of the man through the door in case preparations might be made before I was admitted. It was needless. Almost instantly there emerged a small professor surrounded by several stalwart students who descended the flight of stairs towards me with every appearance of furious hostility.'

'The professor, his raised voice quivering with unbridled irascibility, and flourishing my card aloft in his hand, inquired in choking accents how I dared come there with such a request, and refused me admission in a torrent of incoherent spluttering invective.'

'Much diverted, I waited till he paused for breath and then inquired who might be the person that I had the pleasure to address. Somewhat sobered, he replied that he was Professor Starling; and I re-joined that if he did not wish me to see his laboratory there was an end to the matter, and I bid him goodday and departed, leaving him with rather a dejected appearance of deflation, which was not to be wondered at, for no doubt he discovered too late that he had afforded me just the information I wanted.'

Coleridge's story has the ring of truth. Physiologists— of whom Ernest Starling was one of the most eminent in the world, as was his brother-in-law who worked in the same laboratory, William Bayliss—were not above the use of libel laws to protect their reputations. Indeed, Bayliss had sued Coleridge for libel in 1903 and Coleridge was as unsuccessful a libel defendant as he had been as a libel plaintiff in the case of the reverend Macdonald. (Professor Starling, on the other hand, did not sue for libel after the publication of *Vivisection*, despite the presence of witnesses.)

In the case of Bayliss, Coleridge alleged that Bayliss had broken the law on the use of animals in experiments, and had been cruel to a particular dog, a brown terrier, by operating on it without proper anaesthesia, thus causing it to suffer. Eventually the case was to lead to several small riots by medical students in London, and to the destruction of a monument in Battersea to the dog on whose plinth the libel was repeated (a replacement was erected in 1994 and still stands, for the subject of vivisection continues to arouse deep passions).

Two thousand pounds was awarded to Bayliss (the equivalent perhaps of £200,000 now, though public subscription quickly raised the money on Coleridge's behalf). William Bayliss, the discoverer of hormones with his brother-in-law Ernest Starling (whose 'law of the heart'—physiological not emotional—is still taught to medical students), gave the money to research, so that Coleridge's action had precisely the opposite of that intended.

It took the jury only twenty-five minutes to return its verdict, but it seems to me that its verdict was perverse, and that Coleridge had been substantially right in his allegations that professors Starling and Bayliss had broken the law relating to vivisection under the Cruelty to Animals Act of 1876. Under one provision it stated that experiments on live animals were not to be performed for the purposes of teaching students unless they 'are absolutely necessary'.

Here is part of the cross-examination of Bayliss as reported in the *British Medical Journal*. Bayliss had already answered affirmatively that, where 'you can impart the knowledge without the experiment it is your duty not to perform the experiment.' The experiment on the terrier was designed to show to show to students that the pressure at which saliva is secreted is higher than the blood pressure of the gland's arteries. Bayliss agreed that this principle had long been ascertained for over twenty five years.

Q: Then do I understand you to say that no function of

nature can be properly taught to students without the actual operation on live animals?

A: It would be much better taught. There are many things that cannot be shown in the short space of time at the disposal of a lecturer and the conditions are too complicated.

Q: When you say it could be much better taught, do you mean more impressively taught?

A: Certainly.

Q: But the Act says you are only to do it where it is 'absolutely necessary to the due instruction of the student'?

As Bayliss conceded that, for administrative or economic reasons, not every physiological principle could be taught by experiment, he could not possibly argue that students were therefore ignorant of what they had not been taught in this way. Coleridge's counsel should have won the day.

Bayliss and Starling had broken the law in another regard, too. According to the Cruelty to Animals Act of 1876, an animal that had been used for an experiment under anaesthesia was to be killed painlessly as soon as the experiment's object had been attained. In the case of the brown terrier on which Bayliss conducted his experiment in front of students, Starling had already experimented on it two months before, this time on its pancreas (the research that would found endocrinology). When it had recovered from that, Bayliss conducted another experiment on it. The cross-examination of him went as follows:

Q: Supposing then that this dog had been operated upon by Professor Starling in December, had been examined in February, and the experiment had been completed, was there any statutory duty according to your view of the law to destroy it?

A: The dog was being destroyed: [my] experiment was made on the dog during the process of its destruction.

Q: Then do you say you may kill a dog by inches?

A: The animal was to all intents and purposes dead from the time the anaesthetic was given to it.

It is true that Coleridge's allegations went beyond a simple claim that Bayliss had broken the relevant provision of the Act. Coleridge had stated that the dog, because it had not been properly anaesthetised, had suffered great pain. Bayliss and others testified against this charge, negating the evidence of two anti-vivisectionist women who had gained admittance to his laboratory.

Little wonder, then, that Coleridge came to the conclusion that the cards were stacked against his campaign, that his opponents would stick together, and that official Home Office inspections of laboratories were formalities only, intended simultaneously to reassure the public and pull the wool over its eyes (a little like OFSTED inspections today).

In fairness, Coleridge himself did concede that certain knowledge could be obtained only by experiment on live animals—and that was a price worth paying. The *British Medical Journal* will not publish any scientific work in animals. This, however, smacks of the special pleading so rife in this area; in so far as much of what the journal publishes is ultimately based upon some form of animal research.

---

[1]   When I read this, I was appalled. The most famous son of Les Vans (a town the Ardèche, France) is Léopold Ollier, one of the greatest surgeons of the nineteenth century and the one who invented the bone graft. There is a small but excellent museum dedicated to his life and work in this town, amongst whose exhibits is a statuette of him standing with a mother and child kneeling at his feet in a gesture of profound gratitude. This might seem melodramatic, even absurd, to us. But when one sees photographs of the terrible deformities that people then suffered, and which the pioneering work of Ollier so greatly alleviated, one understands the gesture. But in order to perform his operations, Ollier had first to establish that it was the *periosteum* (the tissue adherent to bone) from which new bone grew. I have in my possession a copy of his paper, *Du perioste au point de vue physiologique et chirurgicale* ('Of the Periosteum from the Physiological and Surgical Point of View'), in which he describes his experiments to prove the osteogenic role of the *periosteum*. I quote: 'I started with the periosteum, which I detached from the bone; first I dissected form the tibia of a rabbit a strip of this membrane 5 or 6 centimetres long, threaded it around the limb between the muscles and the skin, and I thereby obtained bones, or rather prolongations of bones in various forms. I made circular, spiral, cruciform bones, etc., etc.; I was able to give the bone the form I wanted....' It is very difficult to believe that this involved no suffering on the part of the rabbits, but to call Léopold Ollier 'a scoundrel worthy of the lethal chamber' is abhorrent. It is impossible also to believe that this great man was a sadist or motivated by anything other than a desire to alleviate the human suffering. Dr Ollier was aware that he was a great man: my copy of his paper, thirty nine closely-printed pages long, at any rate was dedicated to a Dr Murat (who did not cut the pages and therefore did not read it), and signed 'Ollier' with considerable flourish. All collateral evidence suggests that he was a man of humanity rather than an egotist—unlike Shaw who is now a thousand times more famous than Ollier).

7

Insanity
Paler in the Shade

I did not have as much time among the shelves as I would have liked; my wife does not share my book-worming enthusiasm, which appears in any case to be almost entirely a male one judging by my experience. But I was not quite ready to leave Ludlow yet; in fact, not by any means ready.

I found it altogether impossible to resist *Observations on the Influence of Religion upon the Health and Physical Welfare of Mankind* by Amariah Brigham, M.D., published in Boston in 1835. The combination of the biblical name Amariah, a kind given usually by evangelical parents to their children, and repeatedly having read in medical journals of the health-preserving and dementia-preventing effects of religious observation, led me to suppose that the book would be nothing other than an encomium to the benefits of religious enthusiasm. I was quite mistaken—1835 was not our present time. Dr Brigham's *Observations* is, on the contrary, a catalogue of the harms done to health by religious belief down the ages, as his first chapter—'Of Human Sacrifices'—might suggest.

I knew nothing of Brigham (1798-1849) when I bought the book, but discovered that he had been a distinguished man, among other things, a founding member of what became the American Psychiatric Association and the founding editor of what became the *American Journal of Psychiatry*. He was medical superintendent, first of the Hartford Retreat for the Insane (later known by the unctuous name, The Institute of Living) in Connecticut, and then of the New York State Lunatic Asylum. Among his earlier books is *A Treatise on Epidemic Cholera*, a book that, according to a biographical essay written about him ten years after his death, 'contains little strictly original matter' and 'probably had a limited sale and added little either to the purse or reputation of its author, though much discriminating labour went into it.' In the treatise he appeared to ascribe much of the danger of cholera to the anxiety that it aroused, for 'long and anxious attention to the sensation and feelings of the bowels, will tend to disorder them.'

Dr Brigham was a firm opponent of slavery (his father having been a slave-owner in the state of New York before slavery's abolition there), and he was notable for, among other things, the evidence that he gave in the trial of a William Freeman for the murder of four members of the Van Nest family in Auburn, New York, in 1846.

William Freeman was the son of a slave who had bought his own freedom. His mother was half-native American, and to this fact was attributed Freeman's passionate attachment to a free-wheeling life. In 1840, when he was sixteen—by which time he already had a reputation for being disorderly—he was sent to prison for five years for allegedly having stolen a horse, though the accusation was probably false, an acquaintance having pointed the finger at him to deflect suspicion from himself.

While in gaol, Freeman had an altercation with the 'keeper,' in the course of which the latter struck Freeman on the side of the head with a wooden plank. Thereafter Freeman was almost deaf (his hearing having been defective before), and he came out of prison a much-changed man, being now solitary and taciturn.

Having been wronged and the victim of injustice, he believed himself (not surprisingly) to be owed redress. But he was muddled in his mind. He sought warrants to enforce his desired compensation, but without specifying for what incident and from whom. On the evening of March 12, 1846, he entered the home of the 'respectable' farmer John G. Van Nest, and in a very short time murdered him and three members of his family, including a two-year-old child, by stabbing them with a specially-sharpened knife. He then escaped on a stolen horse.

He was soon arrested and tried. A preliminary hearing was held to decide on his fitness to stand trial and, after it was held that he was fit, a trial of the crime itself. Since there was no doubt that he committed the acts alleged against him, his only defence was that of insanity, and Dr Brigham was his principal witness in both trials. There were many other doctors who testified on both sides of the insanity question, being equally divided between those who held that he was sane and those who held that he was insane. As medical superintendent of the state asylum, Dr Brigham was by far the most experienced of the doctors who gave evidence.

It would be easy to mock some of what Amariah Brigham, M.D., said from our current standpoint. For example, he testified that he could often recognise an insane man just by looking at him, and he pointed to a member of the public attending the trial who, Brigham proceeded to claim with certainty, was insane. There followed a cross-examination on this point by the attorney-general of New York, the son of the former president of the United States, Martin Van Buren, that we would now find hilarious:

Q: Can you name any feature that denotes insanity more than the eye?

A: Yes, the muscles of the face, as I before stated.

Q: But you say they move the features. I enquire whether you can name any one feature that denotes it more than the eye?

A: No one feature distinguishes insanity. It is the play of them that gives the expression.

Q: What constitutes the features?

A: The muscles of the face. They cause the expression and show the operation of the mind.

Q: Has not the nose an expression?

A: Neither the nose or ears are expressive of insanity.

Q: Can you safely answer that no other feature denotes insanity?

A: Nothing but the play or repose of the muscles of the face.

Q: Does any one of them denote insanity?

A: I do not know that any one of them does; but the cheeks, the eyelids, the whole countenance does.

This all seems absurd, and yet I remember doctors older and much more experienced than I telling me that they could 'smell' it when a schizophrenic patient entered the room. What they meant, I suppose, was that an alarm bell went off that was difficult to reduce to words. But in a courtroom to rely on such intuition sounds like charlatanry—which, of course, it sometimes is.[1]

Dr Brigham testified that it was more difficult to detect insanity in a person of colour than in a white, both for personal and physiological reasons. He was personally much more familiar with white madmen; but, in addition, one of the primary signs of insanity was a certain pallor of the face, harder to detect in coloured skin—though Dr Brigham reckoned he detected it in Freeman's case:

Q: If the jury should think it natural for him to become paler in jail, would you attach any consequence to that?
A: My judgment is that negroes do not become paler in the shade.
Q: Why?
A: Because they are not coloured from being in the sun.

And yet, despite all this, Amariah Brigham was an intelligent and humane man, who testified to things I have witnessed myself. For example, he said of the seriously disturbed that 'they will tear their clothes into inch pieces, destroy their beds, and break their bedsteads in a period of time so short, that one could not suppose it possible for them to have done it.' Indeed so; I remember a woman who destroyed not only her own bed but several others before she could be restrained; and one person who ate, or at least swallowed, a not negligible part of his iron bedstead. He also mentioned that the insane may (but do not invariably) exhibit an insensitivity to pain that would be impossible to achieve for others. I recall, for example, a manic woman ecstatically running round a ward, praising the Lord at the top of her voice, with a compound fracture of one of her ankles. After catching and subduing her with the aid of others, I think I felt more discomfort in my own ankle, by sympathetic action, than she felt or at least reacted to in hers.

Dr Brigham's evidence was mostly reasonable and careful. When he dealt with the relationship between acquired hardness-of-hearing and paranoia, he stated that the hard-of-hearing are more prey to it, making clear, however, that hardness of hearing is not in itself a sign of insanity. The same went for a family history of madness; the fact that Freeman's uncle and aunt were mad (the latter described as 'a wandering lunatic') did not mean that Freeman was mad. But when one took the whole history of the case of the defendant, he said, the hardness-of-hearing and the family history counted for something.

As to Freeman's motives, Dr Brigham gave exemplary evidence, all things considered. He did not fall into the trap of circular reasoning (which, as expert witness, I have seen more than once sprung in trials for murder) of arguing he must have been mad to commit the murders and he committed the murders because he was mad.

In all probability, Freeman acted as he did because he believed himself due some indemnity for wrongful imprisonment, quite rightly, but became paranoid on this subject and in all probability thought-disordered as well.[2] His hardness-of-hearing and genetic endowment would have made him more susceptible to this reaction. In killing the Van Nest family, who had nothing to do with his initial imprisonment, he probably thought he was in some way gaining restitution—but this motive is only a surmise. What is there to say with certainty?

When Freeman was first caught, there was an attempt by a mob to lynch him, thwarted by the law officers. Popular feeling in the area at the time would not have countenanced either that he should have been declared unfit for trial or found not guilty by reason of insanity. Yet Dr Brigham considered that Freeman was not fit for trial because he displayed no understanding of or interest in the proceedings, and was consequently unable to instruct his defence attorney. Even after he was found guilty, he did not appear to know what he had been found guilty of. When asked, Amariah Brigham denied the implication that he was unduly predisposed to find Freeman insane because he was opposed to slavery, believed former slaves in general to be ill-treated even in non-slave states, and disliked the death penalty. He thought he was insane on the weight of the evidence.

Despite Dr Brigham's evidence, Freeman was (unsurprisingly perhaps) sentenced to death by hanging. A retrial was granted to him on appeal, however, because of a misdirection by the judge to the jury. But before he could be retried, Freeman died in prison of tuberculosis.

Though it was accepted by all that the primary cause of Freeman's death was consumption of the lungs, the doctors in the case were nonetheless ordered to perform an autopsy and it was Dr Brigham, the most experienced of them, who dissected the brain. It bolstered his view with physical proof. He found that Freeman's inner ear was grossly infected and destroyed, and the temporal bone carious, almost certainly through the infection. The membranes of the brain were thickened, presumably from infection, too, either tuberculosis or syphilis, or both. The end of his report reads: 'In conclusion, I add, that at the time of the trial of Freeman, I was very confident that he was insane, and that the heinous crime he committed was the consequence of mental derangement. I can now have no rational doubt of the entire correctness of that opinion.'

Amariah Brigham was not the only one to come out very well from the trial as an upright, intelligent and brave man, who was prepared to defy popular opinion to stand up for what he saw as the truth. Freeman's defence attorney, William H. Seward, did too. Seward was later to become Abraham Lincoln's Secretary of State, in which post he was singularly successful. His feelings about Lincoln were less than whole-hearted, however, for he believed that Lincoln had wrongfully deprived him of the presidency, which would have been his if Lincoln had not opposed him as the Republican Party's candidate.

There is a mania for finding the worst motives in people—as if only the worst motives could be the true ones. Seward's defence of Freeman has been interpreted by some as political and economic opportunism on Seward's part. Seward, who had been ruined financially by his spell as governor of New York State, needed to recoup his losses and the defence of Freeman might make his reputation as a brilliant lawyer (which it did); but the evidence suggests that he was genuinely concerned by the ill-treatment of former slaves and of the insane. He acted for Freeman *pro bono publico* in more senses than one.[3]

[1]   I was once involved in a case in which a woman was accused of having blinded her own son in one eye by an extraordinary attack on him with a metal pipe. She was of previously good character and nothing else was known against her. Her defence lawyers suspected nothing, but the judge 'smelled' that there was something wrong and demanded a medical examination. Her demeanour was dignified but strangely cold and unconcerned about what was, after all, an assault on her son that was both extraordinary and horrible. I was deputed to examine her and spoke to her for two hours. Her manner was, as before, dignified but strangely cold. It was only at the conclusion of the interview that she revealed that she believed herself directly deputed by God to chastise sin and evil-doing in the world, which was why she struck her son (a sinner) with a pipe and blinded him in one eye. She did not regret it because, if God had not wanted her son to lose one eye, he would not have allowed it to happen: but she was acting under His direct instructions. She was both mad and dangerous; and I was much impressed both by the judge's shrewdness and his humanity.

[2]   People who are psychotic may have speech that seems disorganised to the point of incomprehensibility, with a lack of understandable connection between thoughts expressed, neologisms, etc.

[3]   Although the case was important in Seward's career, Glydon G. Van Deusen, in his very lengthy biography of Seward, does not mention Dr Brigham in his account of the case. Such is the passing glory of the expert witness.

8

Religion
Strange Positions

Among the ill-effects on health of religious beliefs enumerated by Dr Amariah Brigham are delusion and ankyloses of the joints. His strictures against some of the more bizarre practices into which religion may entice people were so strong that, for some time after the publication of *Observations*, he was suspected of atheism. He became pious in later life, and if ever he was an unbeliever he did not say so openly, which presumably would have meant social and professional death. Instead, he hid behind the notion of 'religious progress', analogous to progress in other fields such as sanitation (possibly). He did not fully explain how progress in religion is to be measured or what was the increased knowledge that was required to bring it about, but one suspects that he envisaged the abolition of all organised religion:

'If the opposition of the sacerdotal power is continued, then comes a revolution in the religious world, similar to those in the political, because religious teachers or rulers, have ceased to be in accordance in opinion with the mass of mankind, and the latter must eventually triumph, for the interests of the great mass is not to be sacrificed to that of the few.'

There is something almost Marxist in this view. If the

sacerdotal power does not go quietly, it will be overthrown; and one can imagine a division among religious anti-clericals, similar to that among Marxists, between those who believe the revolution may come about peacefully, by reformist methods, and those who think that it must be by force.

Dr Brigham's view is that true Christianity is little more than an ethical system. 'Christ, by establishing no ceremonies, adapted his system to the whole wide universe, to man in all ages and climates.' But, why bother with the divine at all, then? If Christianity or any other religion is nothing but a superior system of morality, its conclusions can be reached by purely secular reasoning, and the gospel of Christ would be but a Palestinian prelude to the Beatles' song, 'All you need is love'. It is no wonder that Dr Brigham was thought to be a closet atheist.[1]

Though I am not religious, even the chapter on human sacrifice, with which I have had not much do either, had an association for me. 'The people of Dumah… sacrificed a child every year', Amariah Brigham writes. This brought back to my mind something that I was once told as I visited the mangrove swamps of Rivers State in Nigeria. A child was thrown in the creek to the crocodile god once a year, to satisfy the crocodiles' lust for human flesh by a single voluntary sacrifice; voluntary, that is, on the part of local population, not on the part of the child.

Whether this was true or not I had no means of knowing, but in *Fetichism in West Africa* (1904) the American medical missionary to those parts, Robert Hamill Nassau, records: '[O]n the adjacent Upper-Guinea coast, until ten years ago there were human sacrifices to the sacred crocodiles of the rivers of the Niger Delta. In the oil rivers of that same coast there was, until recently, an annual sacrifice of a maiden to the river spirits of trade, for success in foreign commerce.' Is the 'until ten years ago' in his book testimony to the longevity of rumour or of its custom? At any rate, the reverend Nassau continues wryly: 'Treaties with foreign civilised nations have now prohibited this sacrifice, but the maiden has not gained much in the change. Instead of being sacrificed to a brute crocodile to please the spirit of trade, hundreds are prostituted to please brutal, dissolute foreigners.' This sacrifice of hundreds of their maidens will nonetheless have yielded a better result to the Upper-Guinea coastal populace.

Is it possible to trace the decline in the religious belief in a population by the proportion of the religiously deluded? Delusion, though it may retain its form, tends to incorporate the cultural tone of the society in which it appears. I had a patient who believed he was Jesus-Christ-returned-to-earth and many more patients who believed that they were in immediate communication with God, as well as two Haile Selassies in his capacity as the reincarnation of Christ. The two happened to be on the same ward in the hospital at the same time and each could easily see through the ridiculous pretensions of the other, but not, alas, through their own.

Amariah Brigham gives the history of a young man which is all too familiar: 'After he became awakened and converted… he soon became distinguished for his zeal and engagedness, and for his ability in prayer… [and] the praise which his efforts elicited... determined him to commit the whole Bible to memory.' This began to seem too much of a good thing, and 'his mother grew somewhat alarmed.' She felt reassured by a religious teacher, however, who told her that no youth could be too conscientious in his religious duties. But when her son resolved to pray all the time, finally 'mental alienation was perceived by his friends.'

I once had a patient who was brought to me by the pastor of a local Pentecostal church. Their religious services seemed to me, an unbeliever, odd but not actually mad. In the course of these services, congregants would suddenly stand and intone gibberish loudly, apparently under the influence of the Holy Spirit.

The difference between the normal congregants and the madman was that the speaking in tongues was compartmentalised in the lives of the former. Once they had had their say in their incomprehensible verbigeration, they resumed their lives where they left off; and they were very nice people. Originally Pentecostal congregations were far-flung immigrants who shared a religion but not a language. But the madman did not accept that there was a time and place for everything and carried over his religious enthusiasm in an embarrassing way, in circumstances in which it was socially inappropriate.

It was this that persuaded the pastor—consulted by the patient's close relatives—that he was mad. After a couple of attempts at exorcism failed, and the devils inhabiting him had not been cast out by the relevant religious ritual, the pastor decided that medication was needed.

Dr Brigham assumes that it was the boy's religiosity that

caused his madness. But it is hard to prove such a causative relationship. Paranoid delusions are moulded by the environment in which they develop and one could almost write an alternative history of technology using the delusions from which people who go mad suffer. When X-rays were the latest technical miracle, the mad feared they were being constantly X-rayed so that their enemies could see them wherever they were; and today the technology of, or in, delusion has become ever more sophisticated.

When I was working as a doctor in the South Seas, a young woman who had just given birth was brought to me because she had covered herself in her own excrement in an attempt to ward off the evil spirits whom she believed were attacking her. It was the covering of herself with excrement that those who brought her considered mad, not her belief that evil spirits were attacking her. That belief was regarded not only as possible, but likely, or even certain. When she began to behave oddly after giving birth, exorcism, with the agreement of her relatives, was tried by the local witch doctor, but his ministrations failed to work. She grew madder and madder until she covered herself as described, and it was then that she was handed over to me.

She was suffering from puerperal fever, the disease that carried off so many women in Europe in the nineteenth century, and a short course of penicillin put her right. I doubt that this demonstration of the power of medicine had any effect on the general belief in evil spirits, and perhaps rightly so. If her illness was not caused by evil spirits, then its cure would not have proved that evil spirits did not exist in the first place.[2]

Ankylosis of a joint brought about by the prolonged maintenance of a limb in a strenuous and unnatural position is one of the more practical health effect of religious enthusiasm that troubled Amariah Brigham. He mentions Hindus and a Mr Ward who 'saw a young man who had held up his arm until it had become stiff…. He told Mr Ward that he had held up his arm in this manner, for three years.' In fact, Brigham rather understates the problems it leads to.

Once someone from a newspaper known for its large circulation called me to ask whether I could go to India the day after tomorrow, staying only for a day. Naturally I asked the reason for this haste, and was told that it was the Kumbh Mela, a Hindu festival held every twelve years when the Ganges at Allahabad turns for a time into nectar that washes away all the sins of those who bathe in it. Moreover, every twelfth Kumbh Mela is of special import, and this was to be the largest gathering of humanity in the history of the world, with ninety million people expected.

I remonstrated mildly that it seemed odd that the newspaper should have had a hundred and forty-four years' notice of the event but had given me only twenty-four hours' notice. 'We don't work like that,' responded the newspaper's representative who called me.

It didn't matter. I knew from the first that I wanted to go, and would go. It was an extraordinary event, colourful, varied, joyous, and above all reverent. Ninety million Hindus could come together at Allahabad in greater peace than can nine young men in a British pub. On the way from Benares to Allahabad I saw a sight that seemed perfectly to capture the spirit of contemporary India: a holy cow by the side of the road munching quietly on a pile of computer printouts.

In the midst of the unimaginably large throng of humanity I came across a nearly-naked sadhu sitting cross-legged on the ground with one hand held aloft straight-armed and motionless. He had held it thus for thirty years and now, of course, could not move it at all. I was told that this was comparatively mild as a personal sacrifice: in the old days, whenever they were, there were real sadhus who held both arms aloft in this way, not just one.

He seemed to have the respect of all around him when suddenly there burst on the scene a man in western dress who proceeded to berate the sadhu. Why was he leading the parasitic life he led? For what purpose had he incapac-itated himself in this ridiculous fashion? Why should people feed him with the product of their labour, in India above all where most people were poor? What use was he, what good did he do? I regret very deeply that I have forgotten the sadhu's reply, which struck me as at once courteous and, more surprisingly, completely reasonable. As a student, I would have been angered at what I should have seen as the idiocy of it all, but I have become more tolerant and even glad that there is room for sadhus in the world.

As a doctor, Brigham identifies risks everywhere, and as an opponent of organised religion he takes the worst example as the rule. He dislikes the eucharist not only because he finds no biblical justification for it, but because the use of communion wine is dangerous. As evidence he cites a newspaper article:

'"the deep, long swallow sometimes witnessed by the officers of the church when the cup is presented", and state that "reformed drunkards have gone directly from the communion table to the tavern."…. Perhaps they are not exactly correct; still they may be, and if so, they afford additional and strong reasons for discontinuing the ceremony entirely.'

Like the modern epidemiologist, if there are grounds for believing that something may be dangerous to the health of a person collective action is required.

Thus, Dr Brigham has it in for both infant baptism and church bells. He concedes that in warm climates the habit of washing oneself frequently may not only be safe but healthy, and therefore that there can be no objection, at least on health grounds, to ablution for religious reasons; but in cold climates it is quite otherwise. There, 'as everyone knows,' it is dangerous to expose people, 'particularly females and invalids,' repeatedly to cold water. The immersion, however, is only a small part of the danger as 'the exposure of infants to the cold in carrying them to be baptised, is one great cause of this increased mortality'.

As to church bells, Amariah Brigham speculates glumly, 'that the sick are very much injured by the noise of the bells on the Lord's day. I have no doubt that in some instances it has proved fatal.'

No one is more morbidly sensitive to pollution by noise than I. In this, I am very Roderick Usher and silence is my Nirvana. Yet on reading this passage in Dr Brigham I could not help but recall my research, nearly forty years ago, into the history of the hospital in which I was then working, Dalston's German Hospital—now partly grade-II listed with some of its buildings used as affordable housing.

As so often the case with hospitals, it was short of cash, and in the 1840s it needed to raise money. It was the owner of some land adjacent to the hospital through which a railway company wanted to run a railway line. The managers of the hospital—dukes and earls and the like—wanted to sell the land; the hospital physicians were deeply opposed, on the grounds that the noise of the trains would be injurious to patients, 'especially the brain cases.' The managers carried the day, as they always do, and the land was sold. On the night the first train was scheduled to run on the newly-constructed line, the physicians stood vigil to observe the effect of the noise on the patients in the hospital. There was none.

[1]   Dr Brigham was certainly not the only person, or the last, to reduce Christianity to a moral philosophy whose conclusions could have been reached by other means. John Ruskin, in his last work, having been brought up in a strong belief in a supernatural religion, concluded that 'pure religion was in useful work, faithful love, and stintless charity.' God was therefore redundant. Nearly a hundred years later, a bishop of the Church of England, John Robinson, wrote that Christianity 'does not bind us to a particular view of where his genes came from or of what happened to the molecules of his corpse.' What need, then, of Christ at all?

[2]   We assume that belief in such spirits, and consequently in exorcism, has more or disappeared from our own society, and no doubt it is much reduced. But one of my few and invariably unhappy appearances on television concerned the reality, or otherwise, of exorcism. Someone from a television company called me and asked me whether I would be willing to take part in a discussion programme about exorcism. Not having had a television at the time for more than thirty years, I naively supposed that a discussion programme consisted of three or four people sitting round a table and discussing something. It turned out that the television company had invited a large audience to the studio and plied it with drink. Special invitees such as I were placed among it. It was not truth that the company

sought from us, but aggressive and even violent controversy. The compere asked the man sitting next to me his experience of exorcism. He had been a soldier in the Falklands war who had killed people and on his return to civilian life had become violently criminal until he met some exorcists in an evangelical church, who caused him to vomit up a little green devil into a plastic bucket. Once he had done so he changed from being a menace to society to being the kind of person whose greatest pleasure was in helping old ladies across the road. His story told, the compere turned to me and asked me what I had to say about it. I found myself in a difficult dilemma. The drunken audience was clearly in sympathy with this man, and if I was dismissive of him might have thought me a typically arrogant intellectual who despised the views of common people. Besides, it was possible that the man's ridiculous belief had actually transformed his behaviour and any doubt cast would cause him to back-slide. On the other hand, I did not want to appear to endorse so preposterous a notion. In the end I said something completely anodyne, to the utterance of which I had given up an entire evening of my life. But I discovered that the idea of exorcism is not necessarily absurd to at least a number of the population in the first part of the twenty-first century—surely worth knowing.

9

Free Will
Headless Frogs

In certain rural districts it is the custom to speak of a child that has been born out of wedlock as a 'chance-child', and of its mother as having had a 'misfortune'; not that anyone really believes the living event to have come by chance, in violation of ordinary law, without conceivable cause, but it is an indirect way of insinuating that it ought rightly not to have come, and that it is not certain who has been concerned in the begetting of it.

This first sentence proved irresistible to me. Almost a century and a half later—for the book was published in 1883—young women still talk of falling pregnant, or catching a baby, and this not in rural areas but in the poorer parts of large conurbations.

They speak as if pregnancy were a kind of contagious disease, like flu or gastroenteritis, contracted unknowing-ly—a verbal means of denying responsibility that is common to all of us at some time or another. We try to transfer the responsibility for the consequences of our own actions to something outside ourselves, from social forces to neurochemicals, to fate or even chance. '[N]ot that any one believes the living event' to have come about by the operation of any of them, 'but it is an indirect way of insinuating that it ought rightly not to have come about.'

The book, by Henry Maudsley, was titled *Body and Will*. Maudsley (1835-1918) was the foremost English alienist, as psychiatrists were then called, of the second half of the nineteenth century, and he gave a large part of the substantial fortune he earned in his practice to found the hospital that now bears his name, and that has become world famous.[1]

Whatever his other merits, Maudsley was not a talented writer. His prose is as clotted as any Devon cream and it has often been remarked that he is seldom consistent for two pages together. From the first sentence of *Body and Will* it is downhill all the way as far as pleasurable reading is concerned. In the hundred and thirty years of this book's existence—I mean the existence of this particular copy of it—no one (not George A. Browne, not R.H.F, not Brian C. Davies, the three of its previous owners who wrote their names or initials in it) ever read past page 72, about a quarter of the way. I know this for certain because the pages when I bought the book were uncut thereafter. It may even be that no one made it as far as page 72 for people used often to cut the pages far in advance of where they read to. A man who marked its margins with pencil either found nothing beyond page nine worthy of emphasis, or did not read beyond page nine.

The writing is arid, colourless, without any kind of clinical or human illustration that might have enlivened it. Dr Maudsley is the kind of writer who would have made even Armageddon sound dull; he seems to have been born prolix.[2]

I at once formed the ambition to read further in the book than anyone had ever read before, come what may. But, could there be a worse sentence than:

'Any direct deliverance of consciousness at any moment is what it is by virtue of the manifold objective and subjective experiences of the individual, by which had been built up by degrees the mind-nature of which it is the present outcome; and its value, little or much, as true or as false coin, depends upon the character of these antecedent processes.'

I could not help but recall what Somerset Maugham said about reading the verse of Racine, that it takes great fortitude of mind to read much of it while suffering at the same time from dysentery.[3] I cut the pages and reached page 75, further than anyone had ever reached before, and decided that honour had been preserved.

Maudsley treats in the book of the knotty philosophical problem of human free will. He comes down on the side of determinism and says that our belief that we are making free choices is illusory. In this he is at one with modern neuroscience—not in itself an automatic guarantee of truth—that our minds are made up before any decision reaches consciousness. This makes consciousness an epiphenomenon, thunder to the brain's lightning as it were, which is implausible from the Darwinian perspective of which Maudsley was also a proponent. Why would consciousness have evolved if it brought nothing of any importance to the organism that had it?

Maudsley dismisses our experience of freedom—the kind of experience of freedom that induced Dr Johnson to kick the table and say that we know that our will is free, and that was the end of the matter—as being of no evidential value. And he argued that, if human actions were not caused in the same way as all other events were caused, they would remain completely arbitrary and unpredictable. But, in fact, as we are able quite often to predict how people will behave, and therefore they are caused in the same way as other events are caused.

I am not sure, though, that this quite establishes what Maudsley wants it to establish. We behave for reasons, but whether reasons are causes is a question argued over by philosophers. Reasons are certainly not identical to causes, because I can have reasons for doing A and yet do B. In choosing between doing A and B, I may think about the reasons for doing the one or the other.

Only if all this thinking, in all circumstances, is but shadow-play—the real decision-making occurring elsewhere out of the reach of consciousness—can we say that conscious reasons play no part ever in determining conduct. But this is surely implausible. The fact that our reasons for acting in a certain way are the same as anyone else's reasons would explain at least some statistical regularities in human conduct. And I doubt that language of meaning will ever be fully translatable into the language of physics, as Maudsley thinks it will. At any rate, I believe that we are so constituted as hardly to be able to go a few seconds without either moral or aesthetic evaluation, albeit implicit, of our constantly evolving situation and surroundings.

At one point (page 107, well beyond page 75, but as I

cut the previously uncut leaves of the book I glanced forward through some of the print), Dr Maudsley tries to draw far-reaching conclusions from experiments on the movements of a decapitated frog:

'With what admirable purpose then does the headless frog act, howbeit it knows not what it does… Behold proof of sensibility, intelligence and will, may well be the exclamation of those who are not sufficiently mindful that the true mode of viewing the phenomena is not to read into them from a higher experience what is not there, but to read out of them, without bias, what is simply there.'

The interesting word in this latter passage is admirable. Where in the real world is found the quality of being admirable?

A neuroscientist may say that when somebody finds something to be admirable, a certain part of his brain lights up in a scan. But at most this tells us that the subject admires something, not that what he admires is, in fact, admirable. When we say that something is admirable, or good, or beautiful, we do not mean only to report on our attitude towards it—on our inner state. Or merely on the fact that someone or other finds it admirable, or good, or beautiful. We believe, on the contrary, that we are describing a quality of the thing itself.

In this perhaps we are deluding ourselves, but that delusion is inseparable from human existence itself. Whether or not free will exists, we have to live as if it did: that is the best answer I can supply.

Whatever else may be said of Dr Maudsley, it is clear that he emphasised the importance of the unconscious well before another materialist-cum-determinist—Sigmund Freud—did so. Years before Maudsley writes crisply, 'but a very cursory inspection of any one's behaviour suffices to show that there are many energies at work below the threshold of consciousness'.

He continues, still pithily, 'Hence comes the gross and ludicrous illusions to which men often-times fall with regard to their motives on particular occasions, the subtle ways in which they innocently dupe themselves, the signal self-deceptions of which they are sincerely capable.' But then follows: 'An actively conscious state attracts to itself reinforcing energies of consonant vibrations from the infraconscious depths of the character.'

Maudsley, nonetheless, did not so fancifully elaborate on the supposed structure and contents of the 'infraconscious' as Freud did later—unless Maudsley, of course, unfolded a rival theory in the remaining pages of *Body and Will.*

---

1   Though not necessarily more effective in its treatments than other hospitals.

2   In 1860, when he was only twenty four, he published a forty-one-page article in the *Journal of Mental Science* about Edgar Allen Poe. It is unreadably verbose and Maudsley manages to make French literary theorists seem succinct.

3   Determination is not, of course, a virtue in itself. Whether it is, or not, depends on whether the end sought by the determination is a good one. The same goes for bravery and originality.

10

Respect
Our Own Book

Without exception, the books I bought in Ludlow were once the property of Dr Brian C. Davies, a former general practitioner in Knighton, the Welsh border town. He died in January 2009 at the age of eighty seven. I imagine him pasting his bookplate (an Aesculapian staff crossed with two Nepalese kukris, he having been an officer in a Gurkha regiment during the Second World War) into the books, believing them now to be his permanent property—as I believe them to be mine after I bought them, and likewise pasted my bookplate into them. There is no more poignant *memento mori* than this.

Dr Davies, besides being an ardent bibliophile, was an old-fashioned general practitioner for thirty two years in Knighton and its rural surrounds. He was evidently much-loved. In the year of his death a book was published about him, *Dr Davies, His Book*, which went through at least three printings, and consists of fond reminiscences of him, his life, and his work. He was a devoted doctor, on call all night, prepared to answer at any time a request to drive into the wilds in his battered Land Rover (truly necessary in those parts), once returning to Knighton with a body strapped to the passenger seat beside him. He knew everyone in the town and everyone knew him; he was the kind of doctor who followed his patients through the life cycle and grew old with them. He lamented that general practice of his type was a thing of the past, destroyed by ever-increasing bureaucracy.

I had a short experience earlier in my career of this kind of devoted general practice which has now disappeared entirely. I acted as a locum for a doctor in a small country town, with a population almost identical to that of Knighton, in the midst of very appealing countryside. The practice was not single-handed, fortunately for the local population. There were two other doctors to supervise my ignorant efforts. It meant I was on duty one night in three for no extra pay: it was a normal part of the job and was expected of me. I was astonished, gratified, and a little ashamed of the respect I received in the town. If only they had known my lack of experience. But if I went into a shop and there was a queue waiting to be served, I was asked to go straight to the head of it because, 'you must be very busy, doctor.' Old ladies gave place to me when I felt it should be the other way round. The quid pro quo was that I would unquestioningly attend to them at whatever time they felt they needed it, even at night, an access to medical care that they never abused.[1] The three doctors all worked full-time and were supported by their wives who took messages for them and perhaps even gave medical advice on occasion when their husbands were out on their visits. This seems an aeon ago, unthinkable now; but it must have been very reassuring for the local population.

Part of the duties expected of me was the visitation of old people, usually widows, living in isolation in the countryside. These visits were only quasi-medical in nature.

I would take the blood pressure of the old ladies to give the impression of medical purpose before getting down to the real business, which was to take tea with them and have a chat. The tea was always lovingly prepared, with doilies under the sandwiches, and home-made cakes. By the end of a round of such visits I felt as though I should never want (or need) to eat again; but of course it was impossible to refuse. It was obvious that the doctor's visit was a high point of their lives, and they loved to be generous. No doubt these days when such a practice is almost inconceivable, only partly because the number of old ladies has multiplied greatly, home visits like these would be decried as lacking an 'evidence base' in justification for them. Still, I cannot help but think that they preserved health better than many a pill that is prescribed, and that in any case they represented a civilised way of practicing medicine, if not particularly accomplished from the technical point of view. Similar time now spent on an excess of paperwork imposed upon general practitioners seems a step backwards as opposed to progress.

Dr Davies, I think, would have agreed. As I read of him in *Dr Davies* I felt a pang of guilt. He was satisfied with the status of big fish in small ponds. How many of us can say they will have six hundred people at their funeral as there were at his?

---

[1]   A doctor in a city in which I later worked told me that he was once called out as an emergency to a patient. The reason she called him was that she had run out of milk and had very young children to look after. She expected him to buy some for her.

11

Change
A Pugilist at Work

Leominster is only twelve miles from Ludlow, but socially it is a lot further. It is a pleasant old market town, sacked more than six hundred years ago by the last Welsh Prince of Wales, Owen Glendower, but it is much less wealthy than Ludlow. In Ludlow the shops cater to the tastes of those with an assured means; in Leominster to those who have difficulty scraping by at the end of the month. Nevertheless, it has two antiques centres, both cavernous, cold inside even in hot weather, both selling a few books. So we stopped on our way to Brecon.

In the first, I found two books I purchased. The first was a volume of the *Lancet*, in excellent condition from 1828-9, five years after the journal was founded. This volume of eight-hundred-and-twenty-four yellowing and closely-printed pages might seem of interest to medical historians only, but in fact it would only fail to intrigue those indifferent to the human condition.

The founder of the *Lancet*, Thomas Wakley, was a great man, larger than life, and at least as interesting. Of volcanic energy, he was an accomplished boxer in his youth, and liked a good scrap. After qualification as a doctor, and with the financial assistance of his father-in-law, he set up practice in Argyll Street in central London and was soon flourishing. However, there then occurred a dramatic incident that was never fully explained. On the evening of 27 August 1820, Wakley was at home when a man knocked on his front door. The man asked him to see a former patient of his, but also for a glass of cider as he was thirsty. Wakley went to fetch it for him, during which time the man let some accomplices into the house. When Wakley returned with the cider, they attacked him, knocked him unconscious, stabbed him and left him for dead. It is said—though at this interval of time it is impossible to judge—that a bandage he had earlier tied round his head because he had a headache saved his life by softening the blow he received. When he came to the house was on fire and he only just managed to escape. His practice was ruined and, though he set up elsewhere, he was not so successful. It was then that he decided to try medical journalism and in 1823—again with help from his father-in-law—he founded the *Lancet*, which was edited by his descendants until 1909.

Two theories have been put forward in explanation of these events. The first is that Wakley was suspected of having carried out the decapitation of the bodies of the five Cato-Street conspirators. They were revolutionaries who plotted to assassinate the entire cabinet on 1 May, 1820, and were hanged at Newgate Prison before an enormous crowd, some of whom paid handsomely for a good view of the proceedings.

A report in the same year has a masked Wakley (if it indeed was him) sever the head of Arthur Thistlewood as he lay dead in his coffin. 'When the crowd perceived the knife applied to the throat of Thistlewood, they raised a shout, in which exclamations of horror and reproach were mingled. The tumult seemed to disconcert the person in the mask for the moment; but on the whole he performed the operation with dexterity; and having handed the head to the assistant executioner, who waited to receive it, he immediately retired, pursued by the hootings of the mob.'[1] This and the fact that the knife was 'similar to what is used by surgeons in amputation' gave rise to the idea that the decapitator must have been a surgeon.[2] But why, then, Thomas Wakley in particular?

The second theory was that the assailants (who were never caught) did not exist. Instead, Wakley inflicted the injuries on himself and burnt his own house down for the insurance money. Certainly, the insurance company with which Wakley had insured his house and goods and chattels suspected him and refused to pay. Wakley took the insurance company to court, won the case, and received the full amount assured. Later in his career, a rival medical journal accused him of having been an arsonist for the sake of insurance money and Wakley sued for libel, winning substantial damages.[3]

Wakley was a combative man who for much of his career was not only editor of the medical journal that he had founded, but Member of Parliament for Finsbury and coroner for half of Middlesex—each of these jobs being more than enough to keep one averagely industrious man busy. He routinely worked a sixteen-hour day; but also found time to hunt and play host on social occasions. Among the many modernising reforms for which he fought both in the *Lancet* and in parliament were the Anatomy Act 1832 that for the first time gave medical schools legal access to human cadavers other than executed criminals for dissection, and that put an immediate end to macabre business of body-snatching. He also campaigned for the abolition of stamp duty on newspapers; the abolition of flogging in the British army; the exposure both of charlatanry and adulteration of food; the official registration of medical practitioners; the appointment of medically-qualified coroners; the end to brazen nepotism in appointments to London hospitals. It is impossible to learn about his life without conceiving an admiration for the man. He was not one of those oleaginous reformers who thinks that enjoyment can or should be put off until a state of earthly perfection is reached.

The opening pages of this volume of the *Lancet* assures readers that, unlike the magazine's detractors, it would never descend to personal abuse but only to rational and justified criticism of figures in public positions. It then rounds on a Dr James Johnstone's ability 'to accomplish his own humiliation' and ends by noting 'the imbecility of our opponents.'

It is not surprising, perhaps, that Wakley frequently found himself in the libel courts. The most famous of the cases was that of *Cooper v. Wakley*, the first case of medical malpractice and the law. Bransby Cooper was the nephew of Sir Astley Cooper, who was at the time the most famous surgeon in Europe. Wakley alleged in print that the younger Cooper owed his appointment as surgeon to Guy's Hospital to the influence of his uncle. The precise words complained of were that Cooper was 'nephew and surgeon, and surgeon because he is "nephew".'

That was only a part of the alleged libel, however. The *Lancet* at the time paid students who attended surgical operations in the great hospitals of London as part of their training to report on them for the journal. This was part of Wakley's campaign to bring medical practice out into the open and make it publicly accountable. The sensational report of a lithotomy operation (removal of a stone from the bladder) carried out by Bransby Cooper at Guy's Hospital, and which ended in the patient's death the next morning, deliberately cast doubt on Cooper's fitness to be a surgeon. It virtually challenged him to sue, which he did. The report was headed 'The Operation of Lithotomy by Mr Bransby Cooper, Which Lasted Nearly One Hour!'

The patient was a fifty-three-year-old labourer from Sussex, sent up to London by his parish to be operated on. From today's perspective—from any perspective, in fact— the operation was horrible. He was held down and then tied up in a foetal position to give the surgeon access to his perineum, which (without anaesthetic) was then cut. The surgeon normally felt for the bladder stone by sound rather than feel: the grinding noise it made when a metal sound touched it. On occasion the operation lasted less than a minute, but usually about five to eight minutes. Cooper, however, had difficulty locating the stone and took about fifty-five minutes to extract it. During this time, he lost his self-possession and said things like 'I really can't imagine the difficulty', 'It is a very deep perineum', 'I can hear the stone when I pass the sound, but the forceps won't touch it—O dear, O dear!'

It makes one anxious just to imagine the scene, let alone to be in the position of the patient who, not only feeling the agony of the operation but hearing Cooper's expostulations, several times asked him to stop and to allow the stone to remain where it was. Eventually, Cooper found and extracted the stone:

'The stone was laid hold of; and never shall we forget the triumphant manner in which the surgeon raised his arm and flourished the forceps over his head, with the stone in his grasp…. The patient being upon the table, bound, while the operator was "explaining".'

The libel case was a cause célèbre in London, and on the day the trial opened the crowd trying to get into the court was so great that witnesses and jurors had difficulty in entering. Wakley decided to represent himself, while Cooper was represented by Sir James Scarlett, one of the most famous barristers of his day, who later became a notoriously bad-tempered judge with a reputation for unfairness.

I started out reading the case with a strong predilection in favour of Wakley, but the longer I read the more doubtful I became. Wakley called witnesses to the operation itself, who said that the description of Cooper's conduct during it was indeed accurate, and that he had lost his composure as he fumbled around, trying one instrument after another in his panic to locate get hold of and remove the stone. One of the witnesses was so disturbed by what he saw that he left after thirty-five minutes, unable to endure the spectacle any longer. As to the allegation that Cooper owed his position as surgeon to nepotism, however, Wakley produced no evidence at all—except that he (Bransby) and his uncle (Sir Astley) were appointed to the staff on the same day. The powerful and authoritarian treasurer of Guy's Hospital, Benjamin Harrison, said that Cooper would have been selected even if Sir Astley had not been his uncle, a proposition for which there was no evidence for or against either. In his opening address to the jury, furthermore, Scarlett pointed out that Bransby Cooper was a man of wide surgical experience, fulfilling many appointments satisfactorily; that he had been a lecturer in anatomy before he was appointed surgeon; and that, as his uncle's deputy at Guy's, he had often to stand in for the great man while he was occupied elsewhere (as, thanks to his fame as a surgeon, he often was). If Bransby were really the bungler alleged, it was the reputation of Sir Astley himself that would have suffered.

Scarlett called the surgeon who assisted Cooper at the operation, who denied that Cooper had used excessive force during the procedure. Various doctors (including Peter Mark Roget, who later invented the thesaurus that still bears his name) testified that Bransby Cooper was a good surgeon; and this was important because the article implied that the bungled operation was not an isolated occurrence but habitual in London hospitals: 'an affair of family influence, jobbing, and intrigue, is to occasion a cruel and wanton augmentation of human suffering, and to render frequent such heart-rending spectacles as that which was lately exhibited at Guy's Hospital.'

The testimony of one witness for the plaintiff was

extremely damaging to Wakley's case: that of Dr Thomas Hodgkin (the first to describe the disease that bears his name), the most eminent British pathologist of his time. It was he who performed the post mortem on the unfortunate patient, which was attended by, among many others, the *Lancet* correspondent who wrote the article. This correspondent, a J. Lambert, had alleged that the bladder wall had been penetrated, as had the wall of the rectum adjacent to it—proof of Cooper's ineptitude. Dr Hodgkin said in response to Scarlett's questioning, however:

'I am a lecturer on morbid anatomy at Guy's hospital. I should think that the perineum of the deceased, from his size, must have been deep.[4] From the appearance of the parts, I was aware of no other wound, except one from the external surface into the bladder. There was none between the bladder and the rectum. After I removed the parts they were put away, and J. Lambert asked to see them. I, or one of my assistants, took them down for him. I went away. Afterwards, J. Lambert showed me a passage between the bladder and the rectum, and, as I had not seen the passage before, I taxed him with making it. If that had been made recently before death, there would be an extravasation of blood. It is my firm opinion that it was made after death.'

Wakley made no attempt to impugn either the honesty or competence of Hodgkin. A Quaker, Hodgkin was known to be an exceptionally upright and idealistic man and it was inconceivable that he should lie in court to protect a colleague. Scarlett duly attacked Lambert. Was not Lambert paid to report cases, more in fact than he derived from any other source? And did not Wakley earn a large income from the *Lancet*, whose circulation largely depended upon the dissemination of such tales? Moreover, Lambert had been thrown out of other medical schools precisely for such sensationalist reporting. Indeed, when Wakley thought he was in the right (as he usually was) he was clearly not entirely scrupulous in examining his arguments.[5,6]

The libel verdict was a full victory for neither side as the jury found for Bransby Cooper but awarded him only 5 per cent of the damages he was seeking, namely £100 instead of £2000.[7] These damages were not nominal—the equivalent of about £10,000 today—but on the other hand were not ruinous or punitive. Wakley's friends and supporters soon raised a subscription that paid all Wakley's costs and damages, so he lost nothing by the case and certainly gained in fame and reputation.

As for Bransby Cooper, it is said that he never fully recovered from the case (he died thirty-four years later, in 1853, and the age of sixty). He was never a very confident man, perhaps from having long lived in the shadow of his celebrated uncle. Nevertheless, he was made a Fellow of the Royal Society and he published several books, including *Lectures on the Principles and Practice of Surgery*, a treatise on the ligaments of the human body in which he is said to have described more of them than there actually are,[8] a two-volume life of his famous uncle, and a posthumous revision of his uncle's treatise on dislocations.

In the very issue of the *Lancet*, next to the report on the trial, Wakley published a scurrilous attack on Alexander

Monro *tertius*, professor of anatomy in Edinburgh.

Monro was the third of his name and family to be appointed to the chair of anatomy in Edinburgh. In all, the Monro family had held the chair of anatomy for one-hundred-and-twenty-six years by the time *tertius* resigned in 1846. The third Monro, unlike the first two, however, was not a man of distinction:

'His magnitude confers a sort of corporeal dignity on sloth. Accurately measured, he stands about six feet; and is awkward in his movements in proportion to his bulk… The component parts of his frame seem as if they had run wild during their growth, in the indulgence of idleness and alimentary excess… his person being a personification of a luxation,[9] and his gait a civil war of muscular motions… in which a deficiency of motion on one side is compensated for by excess in the other.'

This was all good knockabout fun, yet hardly the stuff of libel suits. But further on in the article came the real allegation:

'Everything about him, his manuscripts, papers, and penmanship, bear marks of this indomitable propensity to slovenliness. I have heard him, during a whole lecture, demonstrate an artery for a vein; confound the *symphysis pubis* with the *symphysis menti*; and read a case nearly to the end, without perceiving that it had not the slightest reference to the matter under consideration.'

Monro, however, unlike many others taken to task in the *Lancet*, and perhaps wisely, did not sue.[10]

The very next issue of the journal reported the terrible scandal in which Edinburgh anatomy (though not

Professor Monro *tertius* himself) was embroiled, when locals William Burke and William Hare murdered Hare's lodgers to sell their corpses for dissection lectures. Their case eventually resulted in a reform of the method of procurement of human bodies by medical schools, such that the abandoned poor and destitute rather than executed criminals (there were far more of the former than of the latter) should be subjected to what was then seen by most of the population as an indignity. Monro *tertius*'s connection with the episode was that it was he who dissected the body of Burke—he was hanged for murder on the evidence Hare had given in exchange for immunity from his admission to sixteen joint murders.

Thomas Wakley and Sir Astley Cooper were reconciled later in life and even became friends. Wakley was serious but light-hearted, and, though he was persistent in reaching his goals, he did not bear grudges. He was acerbic but not malicious. Perhaps Cooper was reconciled with Wakley because he recognised that Wakley had acted out of zeal for the public good against his nephew, but not vindictiveness.

[1]   George Theodore Wilkinson, *An Authentic History of the Cato-Street Conspiracy with the Trials at large of the Conspirators for High Treason and Murder, a Description of Their Weapons and Combustible Machines, and Every Particular Connected with the Rise, Progress and Discovery of the Horrid Plot, with Portraits of all the Conspirators, Taken during Their Trials by Permission, and Other Engravings*, Thomas Kelly, 1820.

[2]   The supposed skill with which Jack the Ripper cut up his victims is always the main reason given for suspecting that Jack was medically-trained.

[3]   This story is reminiscent of that of Dr John Bodkin Adams, a general practitioner in Eastbourne who in 1957 stood trial accused of murdering a rich, widowed patient for an

inheritance (including a Rolls Royce). It was widely believed that he had killed many such patients, but he was acquitted—quite rightly on the evidence presented. After a few years journalists forgot that he had been acquitted, but the supposition that he was a murderer persisted. Several times he was referred to in the prints as 'the murderer Bodkin Adams' and each time sued for libel, and each time won. He died a rich man.

4   Important, because it would have accounted for the difficulty of the operation.

5   In fact, I believe the allegations against Cooper to have been substantially correct. Cooper later published his own account of the operation (reprinted with admirable fairness by the *Lancet*, which, denuded of its emotive language and exclamation marks, was far from incompatible with the *Lancet*'s own report. Moreover, Sir Astley Cooper and other surgeons sat on the bench beside Lord Tenterden, the trial judge, which hardly suggests judicial impartiality—though in his charge to the jury he seems to have been impartial.

6   It is worth pointing out that Thomas Hodgkin did rise under the system to great eminence without any patronage, and that, among his colleagues at Guy's were such physicians as Thomas Addison of Addison's disease and Richard Bright of Bright's disease. James Blundell, who performed the first successful blood transfusion in history, was on the staff also. Sir Astley Cooper, as an anatomist, discovered several structures named after him and also had at least four syndromes named after him. One might wonder just how damaging the system of patronage actually was.

7   One of the corruptions of our civil law is that no inference as to the plaintiff's honesty is drawn from the fact that he has claimed grossly inflated damages by comparison with a more objective measure. Admittedly, where the damage claimed is to reputation and therefore to future earnings, it is not easy to give an accurate estimate.

8   Plarr's *Lives of the Fellows of the Royal College of Surgeons*.

9   The displacement of a bone in a joint.

10   Among Wakley's animadversions in this volume of the *Lancet* are several on the treasurer of St Bartholomew's Hospital, Rowland Stephenson, who absconded to America with the modern equivalent of scores of millions which he stole from the bank in which he was a partner. At the time of his disappearance from British shores he was Member of Parliament for Leominster, where I bought the book. Some are apt to make much of such coincidences: but could a world exist in which there were none?

12

Love
Chien professeur

The editor of my first book told me that the famous publisher Jonathan Cape once said that there were only two things you need to know about publishing. The first is that books about Nelson never make a loss; the second that books about South America never make a profit. My first book was on South America. I suspect, Cape might have added that books about dogs never make a loss either, at least not in England.

Although I love dogs, I am only an intermittent purchaser of books about them. Nevertheless, I must have accumulated about seventy or eighty of such books (my favourite title is *Why Bad Dogs?*—which, I am glad to say, places the blame entirely on their keepers), preparatory to writing a projected philosophical memoir of my dog Ramses. My motive in projecting a book about dogs in general and my dog in particular was not to make money, however inevitable a profit might be, but to raise up some kind of monument. I still painfully miss Ramses, even years after his death, on whose tomb in my garden I still place flowers.

Near to the volume of the *Lancet* that I bought in the antiques centre was an undistinguished volume in blue cloth with the title *Let's Talk of Dogs*. It was by a man called

Rowland Johns, also author, according to the title page, of *Dogs You'd Like to Meet*, and was published in 1930. Johns, in fact, was a prolific author. His titles were intriguing. He wrote a pamphlet on *Dog-Stealing* (1912) and a booklet titled *Edith Cavell, Dog Lover* (1934).[1] Another title, *Lucky Dogs: Stories of Chums of Well-Known People* (1931), had a jacket with a large blue swastika, below and on and in the corners of which sit various dogs. I bought the blue-cloth book (£4) as much for its pencil inscription as for itself: 'To my dear parents Mr and Mrs J.W. Dix', it said, 'with love from their Sealyham son, Bede W. Dix.' The Sealyham is a small long-haired terrier that in Rowland Johns's time was a popular breed but is now so uncommon that it might die out altogether. Johns also wrote a book *Our Friend the Sealyham* that ran to three editions and was one of a series of *Our Friend the…*, each of twelve chapters devoted to a single breed.

The inscription interested me. Was Bede the human son of Mr and Mrs J.W. Dix, pretending to be a Sealyham the better to attract their undiluted affection, or had someone written these words in the name of the Dix's pet Sealyham called Bede, coyly claiming that they were his mother and father? When my wife and I took our dog to the vet, his clinical notes recorded us as his mum and dad, not as his master and mistress or as his owner. I was glad of this, for I do not think that one owns a dog. I dislike sentimentality—except about dogs.

The author's transparent literary conceit in *Let's Talk of Dogs* is that the chapters recount a conversation that his friend, 'John Francis Dolloy', strikes up with strangers in charge of a dog. 'Extraordinary how potent cheap music is', says Amanda in Noel Coward's *Private Lives*, and strange it is how books of no distinction can nevertheless evoke so many associations and memories. 'I've found,' says Dolloy in the first chapter in the book, 'that a lot of folk—even complete strangers—are ready to talk of dogs.'

And so there is. When my wife and I are walking in Paris where she has family, we always stop to talk to people who are walking their dogs and they always have time. There was, for example, the lady in her late seventies in the rue des Pyrénées walking her young apricot poodle that we stopped to pet, who told us that it was he who kept her active and prevented her from being lonely in her widowhood. She had made arrangements for her dog's care by a friend in case of her death before his.

Then there was the *chien professeur* (the teacher dog) in the avenue Gambetta, a bouncing female Jack Russell, a *jolie laide*, who kept jumping up to catch her master's stick that he held up above her head just out of her reach. His master was taught in a school for what used to be called maladjusted children—we change the names of things and phenomena much more easily than transform the things and phenomena themselves. He had discovered by chance that when he took his dog into the classroom the behaviour of the children improved immediately. So now he took the dog with him every day. His observation corroborated mine from my work as GP that much of the ill-conduct of children derives from a lack of affection.

It works both ways, this willingness to talk about dogs. One day we ourselves were walking Ramses just opposite the bois de Vincennes when we were approached by a man in his thirties. He began to talk to us of his dog, very similar to ours, who had died, alas, at the age of seven of kidney disease. He still had not got over his loss, he said.[2]

In the prison in which I worked I found that to talk of his dog established a relationship with a prisoner as nothing else, especially when I talked a little of my own. And prisoners—of whom I remember two in fifteen years—who had been imprisoned for cruelty to dogs had to be protected from the wrath of other prisoners in the same way as did sex-offenders.

Practically every chapter in *Let's Talk of Dogs*—yes, let's, I thought—evoked memories. In a chapter in which a man from the Black Country (not far from where I live) complained on his holidays about a dog on a beach in Wales, how could I fail to remember the first time Ramses ever saw the sea and ran, mad with joy, on the beach at Aberdaron? Or when I read the chapter about a lost chow, how could I not recall my first dog, a chow halfbreed called Chips, whom I loved far more than my parents, and who, when we moved house, got lost and returned, several days of starvation later, to our old address?

Unexpectedly there is a chapter in *Let's Talk of Dogs* that contains a succinct and convincing account of depression from the inside, as it were. Dolloy talks to a man who, to his own surprise, has recently grown fond of a German shepherd.

'When I tried to think out a problem [it] made me think of rats gnawing at my brain. I would sit down and write—that's how I earn my living—and I would conjure up a

character or a landscape and try to make a word-picture
which would convey their beauty to the reader. All the time
I was writing the hideous rats would be nibbling and
munching; I felt like an architect trying to design a palace
on a site which he knew to be a water-logged quagmire
incapable of being drained.'

Then, by chance, he came into possession of his
German shepherd, and the dog cured him. He took him
for a walk on the moors: 'I could not help revelling in
watching him vault over heather-bushes, his delight in his
leaping and running gave me an exhilaration which I had
not felt in a long while.' Ramses, too, was possessed of
what Dolloy's informant called (and it is a memorable
phrase) 'superb happiness.'

Those who write exclusively about dogs are not very
high up in the literary firmament, perhaps. But Rowland
Johns knows about their keepers too. He knows, for
example, that they discuss the absurd and very faintly
disturbing question of whether, if it were possible to
rescue only the spouse or the dog from a fatal situation,
which it would be.[3] And he knows that the dog-lover,
however disbelieving in an afterlife, hopes to be reunited
with his animal after his death.[4] In one of the chapters, a
girl enters an essay competition whose subject is 'What I
Don't Like about Dogs.' Try as she might, she can't think
of anything, and she ends:

> In fact, I've come to the conclusion that the only thing
> I do not like about dogs is that their lives are too short.

¹ Edith Cavell was a British nurse who worked in occupied Belgium during the First World War and treated wounded German and allied soldiers alike. Her most famous utterance was 'Patriotism is not enough.' She was shot by the Germans because she helped many allied prisoners to escape. The fact that she was a dog-lover would have tended to emphasise, emotionally if not in strict logic, both her essential goodness and the particularly heinous nature of her execution. This is not true in every last case, of course. Both Hitler and Ceausescu were dog lovers. A newspaper once sent me to cover Crufts, perhaps the most famous dog show in the world. There I learned of the necessary presence of a forensic veterinarian at the show, to diagnose and if possible prevent the poisoning or drugging of dogs by rival owners desperate for a prize (one dog died of poisoning while I was there). I did not much care for the show as a whole in any case: it seemed to me to use dogs as a prop or boost to the egos of breeders. On the train home from the show I sat opposite a breeder who had shown dogs and we fell to talking. 'I suppose you must love dogs,' I remarked with the exemplary banality of English conversation. 'Not particularly,' he replied. 'For me it's just business.' Although this reply derailed our conversation from its track of predictable cliché, it shocked and horrified me. But there was one breeder at the show whom I had liked, an Israeli woman living in London. She was showing her Dobermans, splendid, sleek creatures, but not a breed one would have associated with the feminine (it was developed by a German tax collector of the name of Dobermann to aid him in his not always popular professional activities). She told me that she had devoted so much attention to her beloved dogs that her husband had finally asked her to choose between them and him. 'I didn't hesitate for a moment,' she replied. 'He had to go. And now, when I am feeling a little broody, I just breed some more.'

² The chapter in which this is discussed is titled 'Save Ruddy First' (Ruddy being the name of a dog).

³ The chapter in which the afterlife of dogs is discussed is titled 'An Old Man's Hope for a Future Meeting with His Dog'.

⁴ The degree to which the two religions are actually hostile to dogs, or rather the keeping of dogs, is a matter of debate within each of them. Nevertheless, the feeling-tone of the two religions (if I may so put it) is hostile; those who argue within them for the permissibility of canine pets are on the defensive; and I noticed that some in the park used to shy away as I walked my dog past them, though he was the friendliest and most unthreatening of creatures to whom small children were instinctively drawn. I noticed also that the mode of argument in the two religions was very similar, deeply scholastic in its constant but quibbling appeal to prior authority, in order to reach a superstitious verdict. The Enlightenment no doubt had its own pitfalls, but I have never felt its vital necessity so strongly as on reading the arguments about dogs by Jewish and Islamic scholars.

13

Suffering
Drought and Leanness

Brecon is thirty miles from Leominster, into increasingly
beautiful and sparsely inhabited countryside. On this route,
one suddenly realises how much of a relief it comes, like
silence after noise, to see little or nothing that was erected
after the Great War. Brecon has a few such buildings, and
monstrous they are too, but they are not large or numerous
enough to ruin all that they survey.

Brecon is on the river Usk, second only in beauty to the
Wye, which my wife never fails to extol as her favourite in
the world, as it is mine. The valley is exquisite in a gentle
and unobtrusive way. We call it nature, but in fact it is the
product of a co-operation between nature and man going
back centuries. It is not so much nature red in tooth and
claw as nature meek and mild, at least until you start
looking more closely, or from the field mouse's point of
view.

Named Aberhonddu in Welsh, it is a small town—or
rather city, since it has a small and rather squat grey stone
cathedral, raised to that ecclesiastical dignity in 1923 after
the disestablishment of the church in Wales—and is not
rich. We stayed overnight in a simple bed-and-breakfast
where I experienced a sense of relief. A bare room—a
chair, a bed and a table, and nothing else. This is the way to

live, not as I have been living, and I recall the bedroom painted by Van Gogh, luxuriously bare, and wish it were mine. Of course the mood does not last. After all, there is an interesting second-hand bookshop, and I know I will depart with more possessions than I arrived with.

Brecon's literary spirit is Henry Vaughan, poet and country doctor of the seventeenth century. His tombstone in St Bridget's churchyard, Llansantffraed, claims that he was a doctor of medicine, though no one has ever discovered how he came by his degree. John Brown, in his essay on Vaughan in *Horae Subsecivae*, a collection of articles on medical history, says that the degree was granted in London, but if so it must have been by the archbishop of Canterbury, who was the only authority in London at the time with the power to grant such a degree. What is certain, however, is that Vaughan practised as a doctor in Breconshire with some success, and even translated medical treatises into English, a language, as his twin brother, Thomas, put it, he was not born to—Welsh being their maternal tongue.

These treatises are not without interest still for—as the translator says 'to the ingenious reader' in his preface—'in my owne part, I honour the truth where ever I find it, whether in an old, or a new booke... I wish we were all unbiased and impartiall learners, not the implicite, groundlesse proselyts of authors and opinions, but the loyall friends and followers of truth.' And among the individual truths enunciated by the author through his translator are those about diet, never more salutary than in this age of obesity: 'whence follow frequent and unwholesome evaporations and belchings, which so fill and oppresse the vessels and organs of the spirits, that they are hindered in their functions.'

But Vaughan, the Swan of Usk, is known rather as a religious poet. Religious poets do not take the world for granted, but are grateful for its existence—that there is something rather than nothing—and therefore never express that disillusionment that has never known (or admits to) illusion in the first place. It was serious illness, or rather recovery from it, that turned Vaughan religious, like a heart attack makes a man give up smoking where nothing did before: 'for,' says Vaughan in the preface to his book of religious poems, 'I was nigh unto death', to which he added 'and am still at no great distance from it.'

For the religious, it is an appealing thought that there is more to suffering than meets the eye:

… Suffering, then, has its purpose:
Were all the year one constant Sunshine, wee
Should have no flowres,
All would be drought, and leanness; not a tree
Would make us bowres…

On our way to the centre of Brecon from the bed and breakfast, we passed the Henry Vaughan Health Centre, and I thought that, while suffering as such may be inescapable and even salutary in a human life, a doctor would be very strange who, confronted by his patient's suffering, offered: 'Were all the year one constant Sunshine.'

In the centre of Brecon is Bethel Square, which is dominated by the large, neo-classic grey-stone Bethel Chapel belonging, formerly, to the Calvinistic Methodist Church. The chapel, built in 1852, is now known as Unit 8, Bethel Square. It was converted into a large pharmacy in the 1990s, the chapel having fallen into disuse in the previous decade. From the care of the soul it has transitioned to the care of body, or even just of the face—any modern pharmacy is above all an emporium of cosmetics.

I do not know whether to celebrate or lament the sudden collapse of Welsh religion. At the time of my father's birth in 1909 the Calvinistic Methodist Church, a Welsh denomination, had more than fifteen hundred chapels, all of them well-attended. Chapel life still appeared to be vigorous, an inextinguishable feature of Welsh life, when he owned a factory in Tonypandy in the Rhondda Valley. Nowadays, practically all the chapels in Wales—not just of that denomination—have been either abandoned or converted into spacious houses, shops, or even nightclubs.[1] The religious collapse has been even more complete than that of Catholicism in Ireland.

On the one hand, the religion always seemed dismal in the extreme—obsessed by the fear of the morally-corrupting nature of ordinary pleasures, with a view of life as slate-grey and rain-sodden as most of the chapels themselves. I was younger than ten and still remember Sundays in Wales when, as a visitor, it was hard enough to find anything to eat, let along to drink. The desire to eat was regarded almost as if it were a manifestation of moral degeneracy, the first step on the slippery slope towards whoredom. After all, a respectable person would have been at home between chapel services, not gadding about in search of amusement.[2]

On the other hand, the chapel and the life that centred on it had a very strong and distinctive flavour of its own, which has now been dissipated in the homogenising mediocrity of modern consumerism. Unit 8, like Units 1, 2, 3, 4, 5, 6 and 7 of Bethel Square, is occupied by a chain store exactly uniform as to decoration and stock with that to be found in any town in Britain. Wales, Norfolk, Hampshire, Cumberland, wherever, it is all the same. There is even the ubiquitous charity shop, nowadays the most characteristic British institution, in Bethel Square—in this case Oxfam.

The old non-conformist conformism of Wales inspired writers like Caradoc Evans and Rhys Davies, not much read now through no fault of their own. They were clear-eyed about the censoriousness, hypocrisy and even cruelty of the chapel-centred way of life, its joylessness and its severe aesthetic limitations, its highest aesthetic achievement being the choral singing of hymns. And yet, strangely enough, the characters it produced seemed far more interesting and individual than those who have resulted from its overthrow. Rhys Davies wrote of that way of life with amusement and a Chekhovian tolerance and understanding, rather than with bitterness. Nonetheless, I note that he escaped to London as soon as he could and went back to South Wales only for short visits.

Our civilisation at the time was founded, as George Orwell once remarked, on coal, without which we would have lived in unlit and unheated houses. The miners were like Atlases; upon their shoulders a whole world rested. My visual recollection of Tonypandy is monochromatic—of everything begrimed with coal dust; of the slate roofs of tiny terraced houses dull in the perpetual, dirty rain; of black slag heaps lowering over the town. Whether this is a true memory or a reconstruction based on what I subsequently learned, I could not swear in a court of law.

My father always disparaged the character of the Welsh, for whom I therefore conceived an affection that has remained with me ever since. If one can be a patriot of a country not one's own, I am a Welsh patriot.

[1]   It is not difficult to find lists of chapels for sale in Wales, suitable for conversion—a term more used nowadays by estate agents than pastors—to 'heavenly' homes.

[2]   The dog-in-the-manger attitude to pleasure of Welsh religion is succinctly captured in the only specifically Welsh joke that I know. A young man asks the preacher whether it is permissible to have sex on Sundays. The preacher thinks for a moment and then replies, 'Yes, so long as you don't enjoy it.'

14

'I feel it more.'
D.H. Lawrence

I approached the second-hand bookshop in Brecon with the kind of mounting tension that I assume the drug-addict feels as he goes to meet his dealer. I sense a stirring that I would describe as a compulsion to buy a book, though I know perfectly well that it is nothing of the kind. That I can help myself if I want to, and would not resort to crime if I were without enough money to buy one.

Nowadays when you are in search of a particular book, all you have to do is look it up on the internet and it arrives through your letterbox a few days later. There is no excitement or achievement in it. The pleasure of browsing in a shop is the possible discovery of something that you never knew existed and fires your imagination.

As I entered the shop, I was immediately greeted by, or rather my eye fell immediately upon, a familiar sight. The familiar sight was that of a first edition of a D.H. Lawrence in the uniform brown cloth covers given to his books by his British publisher, Martin Secker.

It was the commonest and therefore the least expensive of Lawrence first editions, the novella *The Virgin and the Gipsy*, which I had never previously bought or read, though I saw the film when it was released in 1970s. Lawrence in those days was still regarded as a liberating force and somewhat uncritically admired. I found him overblown and even ridiculous. Since then, however, I have come to admire his poetry and grown more sympathetic to him as person—no one could remain unmoved by his extraordinary trajectory in life or the mode of his death—so that by a strange irony, when his books were in every bookshop I thought little of him and now, when he seems an almost forgotten figure except perhaps as grist to the mill of academic industry, I find myself drawn to him.

There is no disguising that *The Virgin and the Gipsy* shows him at his very worst, and his worst is bad. It was published in the year of his death, 1930, but posthumously, from an uncorrected manuscript. Perhaps he would have had the sense not to publish it at all, for it seems to me a hybrid of Barbara Cartland and Alfred Rosenberg. The book begins:

'When the vicar's wife went off with a young and penniless man the scandal knew no bounds. Her two little girls were only seven and nine respectively. And the vicar was such a good husband.'

The plot is a simple and implausible one. The frustrated daughter of a rector in the North of England meets a sultry dark handsome gypsy and is attracted to him. Later she is rescued by him when a nearby dam breaks and a tidal wave floods the rectory, after which he makes love to her and then disappears. He symbolises authenticity and, in some Lawrentian technical sense, life, and is in complete contrast to the deadness of conventional existence at the rectory.

Being a good husband is here an accusation rather than

an encomium; but I am conventional enough not to think that the abandonment of two young children by their mother, apparently to satisfy herself and without so much as a moment's consideration for their welfare, is other than reprehensible.[1] Throughout the book, indeed, the rector's wife is taken as a symbol of emotional honesty, though never once does she so much as enquire after her two daughters, let alone visit them.

In my medical career I encountered much abandonment of children by parents who found that they disagreeably constrained their freedom. Fathers abandoned their offspring far more readily than mothers, of course, but abandonment by mothers was far from unknown, and I remember one mother who put her fourteen-year-old daughter out onto the street because she wanted her new boyfriend to move in.

I suppose Lawrence would have defended himself against the charge that he was an apostle of such behaviour by pointing out that the two daughters in *The Virgin and the Gipsy* had a perfectly secure and comfortable home provided by their father, and that therefore their abandonment by their mother was not to be compared with the case I have just cited. True enough that the case is not as bad. Material circumstances make an important difference. But it would be a very crude view of a child's needs that a warm bed and a dry roof justify and fully compensate for such behaviour.

There is an unpleasant kind of *Blut und Boden* (Blood and Soil) philosophy lurking not far beneath the surface of this book. The instinct of the farmyard is glorified at the expense of the artificial refinements of conventional and above all bourgeois society,[2] and blood, whatever that may mean, is exalted over brain. Race is very important as an explanatory category in Lawrence's mind. The gipsy is as he is (that is to say, smouldering away in sultry fashion) because he is a member of an ancient race; and because of his blood, therefore, he would have smouldered away just as strongly if he had been brought up in Esher or Winchester. Yvette believes that all her father's family are 'low-born,' not in the social but in the racial or biological sense. They are constitutionally inferior, however socially prominent they may be.

It is not altogether surprising that the book contains some mildly disconcerting anti-Semitism. Lawrence wrote as early as 1908:

'If I had my way, I would build a lethal chamber as big as the Crystal Palace, with a military band playing softly, and a cinematograph working brightly; then I'd go out in the back streets and main streets and bring them in, all the sick, the halt, and the maimed; I would lead them gently, and they would smile me a weary thanks; and the band would softly bubble out the "Hallelujah Chorus".'

This was an odd thing for a man to write (even making allowances for his young age of twenty three) who was soon to adopt a pacifist stance during the Great War.[4] As to the sick, he was, through no fault of his own, soon to join them and indeed to endure his sickness with dignity.

While Yvette visits the gipsy in his encampment, a couple who are passing by arrive and want to warm their hands by the encampment fire. The male of the couple is

an athletic blond man whose name, perhaps not coinciden-
tally, is that of the mining village in which Lawrence was
born, Eastwood. The woman is someone whom Lawrence
persists in calling throughout the book 'the little Jewess,'
although her name, Mrs Fawcett, is known almost from the
first. She is rich and sensual, by no means an altogether
unattractive figure, but also: 'The Jewess searched his face
with the peculiar bourgeois boldness of her race.' Actually,
Mrs Fawcett is introduced into the story as only 'probably
a Jewess,' but within half a page all doubt is extinguished.

This pales before another kind of chilling undercurrent,
however, which is evident also in *Lady Chatterley's Lover*. In
Lady Chatterley, Sir Clifford Chatterley has been injured in
the war and is paralysed from the waist down. This
paralysis is obviously intended to be symbolic of more than
just physical incapacity, as if Sir Clifford were responsible
for his own paralysis (which he can only be by way of
collective responsibility of his social class for the war in
which he was injured) and as if it were somehow the
expression of his deepest character. There is not a single
expression of understanding, let alone sympathy, for his
predicament; and this, it seems to me, indicates a true
coldness of heart.

In *The Virgin and the Gipsy*, Yvette lives at home with,
among others, her grandmother, granny (or *mater* to her
son, the rector). Granny at the end of the book is nearly
ninety years old, hard of hearing, and blind. She is also a
domineering, snobbish, killjoy, censorious old crone who
symbolises for Lawrence the bourgeoisie.

When the tidal wave strikes the rectory, granny is at

home: 'Yvette… saw Granny bob up. Like a strange float, her face purple, her blind blue eyes bolting, spume hissing from her mouth. One old purple hand clawed at a banister rail, and held for a moment, showing the glint of a wedding ring.' After the waters have receded, a man from the village climbs in at the kitchen window, 'He found the body of the old woman: or at least he saw her foot, in its flat black slipper, muddily protruding from a mud-heap of debris.'

She got what Lawrence thinks she deserved, as would all 'the sick, the halt, and the maimed' have got it in his fantasy of 1908. Even allowing for the fact that by the time he wrote this book Lawrence was desperately ill and severely handicapped himself, and therefore may have projected his hatred of disability by his depiction of granny, these passages indicate an almost psychopathic coldness of heart.[4]

I couldn't help but compare granny with another resident widow, Dickens's Mrs Gummidge:

Mrs Gummidge had been in a low state all day, and had burst into tears in the forenoon, when the fire smoked.

'I am a lone lorn creetur', were Mrs Gummidge's words, when that unpleasant occurrence took place, 'and everythink goes contrary with me.'

'Oh, it'll soon leave off', said Peggotty, 'and besides, you know, it's not more disagreeable to you than to us.'

'I feel it more', said Mrs Gummidge.

Even if Mrs Gummidge had not turned up trumps later

in the book, one would have sensed from this passage alone the warmth in Dickens's heart, his love of human comedy, his tolerance of imperfection, his glorying in the expressiveness of language.

[1]   'How beastly this [bourgeois] house is!' exclaims Yvette at one point, bringing to mind the famous lines of Lawrence's poem:

How beastly the bourgeois is
Especially the male of the species—

[2]   Likening all bourgeois to 'mushrooms, all wormy inside', Lawrence concludes:

What a pity they can't all be kicked over
Like sickening toadstools, and left to melt back, swiftly
Into the soil of England.

This is, in effect, in invocation to genocidal-style violence.

[3]   No one can dispute the possibility or danger of over-refinement; but it seems to me that, nowadays, under-refinement presents the greater danger, at least in England.

[4]   Bertrand Russell, another pacifist during the Great War, describes in his *Autobiography* how he fell for a time under the influence of Lawrence's extraordinary personality, whose principle characteristic was the burning nature of his conviction that he knew what life was about and how it should be lived. Russell, however, who himself was no stranger to odd political convictions from the need for America pre-emptively to destroy the Soviet Union with nuclear weapons to the unique wickedness of the United States, soon saw through Lawrence and came to the conclusion that his ideas were both horrible and dangerous. Interestingly, Russell saw through Lenin as soon as he met him.

[5]   Is it not also significant that the lack of any sympathy for Sir Clifford (though he by no means an evil man) usually escapes notice? One is almost tempted to propose a law of the conservation of callousness: that if a callous attitude to one group of people ceases, it will soon attach to another.

15

Politics
Trinidadian Oranges

Two feet away from the book by Lawrence was another in
a brown cloth cover, slightly lighter in shade, by Aldous
Huxley—*Beyond the Mexique Bay*, published in 1934. It
recounts a journey he made to Guatemala and Southern
Mexico the previous year, the year after he had published
the work by which he achieved immortality, or at any rate
such immortality as literature can confer, *Brave New
World*—though I have never read anything by him that did
not repay the reading.

Having lived in Guatemala for nine months to write a
book about the revolutionary wars that were then
convulsing the Central American isthmus, I had
accumulated quite a little library on the country which,
strangely, did not include Huxley's travelogue. In my book
I took the unfashionable view that the revolutionary
movements were not the spontaneous protest of the
downtrodden peasantry but the consequence of the
expansion of the universities, and that the victory of those
movements was neither inevitable nor desirable, however
badly the countries had been governed from the time of
their independence.[1]

Thanks to its revolutionary civil wars, Central America
in the 1980s achieved an importance in the minds of intel-

lectuals in Western Europe and North America that it has never had since. Interest has waned to the point almost of extinction. In its heyday, though, a well-stocked bookshop had at least a shelf, and usually more, of books devoted to the future being carved out in *la dulce cintura de América,* the sweet waist of America, as the Chilean poet Pablo Neruda called it, all of them sympathetic to the guerrillas. (And, if Jonathan Cape's rule of thumb was right, none of them a success.)

Oddly enough, Huxley points out in his book the tendency of Western intellectuals to project on to others their deepest longings, or at least their deepest longings in theory—for once you have tasted physical comfort, you are reluctant to give it up for longer than a short period:

'The Mexico of the Indians is more, for these writers, than a mere geographical and sociological reality; it is a place where wishes are fulfilled, and the intolerable evils of the civilised world corrected.'

The projection by intellectuals on to other people and cultures of supposed virtues or charms that they and their own culture do not have is a permanent temptation, permanent because there is often an element of truth in the projection. But only an element. I remember once being in a bar in Skye, a long time before the bridge to the mainland was built, extolling and envying the beauties of the Highland life. 'You should be here in f...en February,' said a local who heard me.

Huxley, in fact, does not seem much to care for the natives, finding them as inscrutable as reptiles, to whose eyes he compares theirs not once but several times. He finds their syncretic religious beliefs completely mystifying. Like him, I watched Indians gesticulating, sometimes almost threateningly, to images of saints in a cloud of copal incense in rococo colonial churches in remote highland villages or towns and wondered what was going through their minds.

Huxley hardly likes the Ladinos (those of mixed European and Indian descent) better, for they, however impoverished or humble themselves, have an absurd and arrogant pride in at least not being Indian. Having someone to look down on is a great consolation in life, especially in a life in great need of consolations.

Nor does Huxley much care for the Europeans with whom he sailed from Europe on board a liner. For example, there is 'a stout lady of mature middle-age' on the ship furiously riding a mechanical horse, presumably to dis-embarrass herself of excess flesh:[2] 'The mechanical quadruped heaved its wooden loins and rhythmically all the superfluous adiposity of its rider lifted and with a jellied shuddering subsided, lifted once more and subsided, again and again, endlessly.' The passengers on board ship are mainly upper-middle class, still moneyed at the height of the Depression, and most of them are elderly.[3] The trip makes Huxley speculate presciently on the year 1980:

'The birth-rate will have declined and the average age at death have risen. This means that there will be a consider-able decrease in the numbers of children and young people, and a considerable increase in the numbers of the middle-aged and old. Little boys and girls will be relatively rare; but men and especially women (since women tend to live longer than men) of sixty-five-years old and upwards will be correspondingly more plentiful—as plentiful as they are on a cruising liner in 1933.'

When the ship calls on Trinidad *en route* for Puerto Barrios, the harbour on the short Guatemalan coast of the Caribbean, Huxley makes another observation that could have been written today. He notes that Trinidadian oranges are of particularly good flavour, but 'they have a complexion which nature has made, not orange, but bright green, irregularly marbled with yellow. Nobody, therefore, outside their countries of origin, will buy them.'

'The appeal of bright colours, symmetry and size is irresistible. The sawdust apple of the Middle West is wonderfully red and round; the Californian orange may have no flavour and a hide like a crocodile's—but it is a golden lamp; and roundness, redness and goldenness are what the buyer first perceives on entering the shop. Moreover, both these fruits are large; and greed is so simple-minded that it always prefers food in large chunks to food in small chunks—prefers it even when the food is being bought by weight,[3] and it makes no difference whether the individual portions are big or little.'

There is a long and irrelevant digression in *Beyond the Mexique Bay*. The stimulus to this digression, which lasts more than forty pages, is Huxley's sight in Guatemala City of Guatemalan soldiers, smartly turned-out and very disciplined, though without any clear enemy to fight against.

The problem of war, says Huxley (a convinced pacifist), is that man needs to express strong emotions for their own

sake—not continually, but from time to time. War satisfies
this need for expression of strong emotions, the need
being as much a part of human nature as are eruptions a
part of volcano nature. Huxley delineates the passions
which must be mitigated if war is to be avoided: 'hatred,
vanity and the nameless urge which men satisfy in the act
of associating with other men in large unanimous droves.'
He writes of hatred as if he were very familiar with it:

'Hate is a spiritual passion, which no merely physiological process can assuage. Hate, therefore, has what lust
entirely lacks—persistence and continuity; the persistence
and continuity of purposive spirit... there is nothing to
prevent the pleasures of hatred from being as deliciously
enduring as the pleasures of love in the Muslim paradise.'

Surely anyone who looks into his own heart will
acknowledge that hatred is the strongest of political
emotions, is enjoyable, and can ambush us at any moment.
No doubt there are some people who are completely
immune from it, but at the other end of the spectrum there
are those who feel little else, most of us falling between the
two extremes in this as in everything else.

Huxley the pacifist does not throw up his hands in
despair and announce that conflict is inevitable. His
solution? Expressions of collective or mass hatred can be
neutralised by mass distractions, organised by psychologists
who can understand and manipulate their fellow beings.
'Benevolence is tepid: hatred and its complement, vanity, is
stinging hot,' which is why 'National Socialism is so much
easier to popularise than the League of Nations.' To this
end, Huxley proposes a World Psychological Conference in

place of the futile disarmament conferences and peace pacts that were a feature of the age.

Another fly in the ointment is education:

'Universal education has created an immense class of what I may call the New Stupid, hungering for certainty, yet unable to find it in the traditional myths and their rationalisations. So urgent has been this need for certainty that they have accepted (with what passionate gratitude!) the pseudo-religious dogmas of nationalism.'

Therefore, 'one of the tasks of the delegates will be the devising of a mythology and a world-view which shall be as acceptable to the New Stupid as nationalism and as beneficial as the best of the transcendental religions.'

It is clear from all this that Huxley's attitude to what he depicted in *Brave New World* cannot have been entirely condemnatory. The main difference between *Brave New World* and what he proposes in *Beyond the Mexique Bay* is that in the latter the population is to be divided into only two strata instead of several: the alpha pluses (a tiny minority) and the epsilon minus semi-morons (the vast majority).

Huxley is a great generaliser, and it is hardly surprising if his generalisations fail on the spot. For example, of our appreciation of nature he writes: 'Nature worship is the product of good communications. In the seventeenth century all sensible men disliked wild nature.'

I thought of the simple lines of Brecon's tutelary literary spirit:

If Eden be on earth at all
It is what we the country call.

For Vaughan, the Swan of Usk, the beauties of seventeenth-century Brecknockshire never paled; and he, who had known Oxford and London, and therefore was no bumpkin, was content to live and die where he was born, buried in the parish where he had been christened seventy-four years earlier.

---

1   My theory of the relationship between the expansion of the universities and the revolutionary ferment was as follows: traditionally, a university education in Central America was both a sign of and a guarantor of belonging to a politico-economic elite. When, under the pressure of modernisation, the universities were expanded, a university education retained the connotation of belonging to an elite but not its denotation, for now there were simply too many graduates for the society to accord elite positions. Bitterly disappointed and disillusioned, the students and alumni, or some of them, turned to revolution as the means of obtain the prominence in society to which they thought their education entitled them. When I visited the University of San Carlos in Guatemala City—Aldous Huxley does not touch on universities in his book—it was like an armed revolutionary camp, which in a sense is what it was. Thanks to its extraterritorial status, typical of the universities of Latin America (no agent of the state, including the police and the army, might enter, though the state was the paymaster of the university), revolutionary extremism flourished, as did the hoarding of arms, and every available surface was covered in revolutionary slogans. Inside the university, the revolutionaries ruled by intimidation; once they left it, physically, they were subject to the full force of the repressive apparatus. It was a kind of academic freedom for revolutionaries tempered by assassination and disappearance without trace. Incidentally, the most vicious of all Latin American revolutionary movements, *Sendero Luminoso* (Shining Path), the Peruvian Khmer Rouge, was the brainchild of Abimael Guzmán, the professor of philosophy at the recently re-opened University of Ayacucho, whose doctoral thesis had been on space as a categorical concept by Kant.

2   'Adolescents of five-and-forty abound,' he says.

3   One of the themes of *Brave New World* is the shallowness of what produces mass contentment. Huxley also wrote a short book on vulgarity in literature.

16

Causality
Kindred Delusions

When Huxley left Guatemala, he went to Oaxaca in Mexico, whose literary guide, at least for Anglophones, is none other than D.H. Lawrence. He was only three years dead when Huxley exposed the bogusness, of Lawrence's philosophy:

'[I]t is significant that he spent only a few months in Mexico and that, whenever he lived among primitives, he found it necessary, in spite of the principles he had made his own, to refresh himself by occasional contacts, through books, through civilised men and women, with the lilies of the mind and spirit. [Yet he thought that w]hen man became an intellectual and spiritual being, he paid for his new privileges with a treasure of intuitions, of emotional spontaneity, of sensuality still innocent of all self-consciousness. Lawrence thought that we should abandon the new privileges in return for the old treasure.'

Seventy years after Lawrence had done so in 1925, I stayed in 'his' Hotel Francia in Oaxaca. I suppose my desire to stay in that particular hotel—it had a kind of luxurious simplicity still—had an element of magical thinking about it. Some ghostly emanation of Lawrence would lend a superior quality to what I wrote. The subsequent fate of my book suggests, in any case, that it did not work sufficiently to deflate Jonathan Cape's prediction.

While on the subject of books with brown-cloth covers, I must mention a very small volume with exceptional quality boards, published in 1928—the seventh edition of *On Colds, Hay-Fever and Influenza* by John Henry Clarke, M.D. Dr Clarke was also the author, in 1915, of *Gunpowder as a War Remedy*, recommending it as an all-round cure 'for blood poisoning in general and septic warwounds in particular'. So small was the book I held in my hand that I might easily have overlooked it, but I am glad that I did not. The author, a consultant physician at the Homoeopathic Hospital, tells us on page 4 that, while a cold may not be a fatal disease in itself, it can nevertheless drive a man to suicide:

'It [the depression caused by colds] is sometimes quite terrible. Life is not worth living for them; and I should not be surprised if the true explanation of the many inscrutable cases of suicide we read of in the papers was not to be found in this as, at least, a partial cause. When the combined wisdom of jury and coroner can assign "no cause for the rash act", it might help them to ask whether the deceased had not had a severe cold in the head at the time.'

Well, if you can believe that, as the Duke of Wellington replied to the man who approached him with, 'Mr Jones, I believe', you can believe anything. Any doctor who can convert to the doctrines of Samuel Hahnemann, the founder of homoeopathy, is already halfway or more to believing anything. 'Convert,' by the way, is the word used repeatedly by qualified physicians to describe how they became homoeopaths, as if they do so as the result of a religious experience.

Try as I might to enter imaginatively into a mental world other than my own, it is still a matter of incomprehension to me that anyone could ever have taken Hahnemann's system seriously. Oliver Wendell Holmes's attack on homoeopathy, carried out as early as 1842, the year before Hahnemann died—in a lecture *Homoeopathy and Its Kindred Delusions* in Boston—was already so devastating that, if the world were ruled by reason alone, the creed would have disappeared once and for all.

Holmes (1809-1894) was a most remarkable man, a man of genius or near-genius. It was he who coined the term 'anaesthesia' for the newly discovered phenomenon. Hahnemann's most famous tenet was that *similia similibus curantur*—that medications that produce the same symptoms as an illness (and no others) cure that illness. Holmes drily remarked that if that were the case, the treatment of arsenic poisoning would be arsenic. As Hahnemann claimed that homoeopathic treatments grow stronger the more and more dilute they become, Holmes pointed out that it would take the whole of the Caspian Sea to contain a very small quantity of the active substance in Hahnemann's 'strongest' dilution.

In case anyone should imagine that this battle is over in our own scientifically-enlightened age, I will just mention that the *British Medical Journal* recently sent me two articles for my comment, one in favour and one against the public provision of homoeopathic treatment, and asked me whether they should be published. The article in favour of the provision of such treatment used precisely the same form of argument that Holmes had exposed more than a hundred and seventy years previously. I recommended publication because it was so bad in an instructive way.

Why should homoeopathy have survived, no matter how ridiculous its doctrine? I suppose the first answer is that it, alone of all medical doctrines, complies with the most basic of Hippocratic injunctions to practitioners, namely to do no harm, at the same time as satisfying our deep desire for cures. But I think there is more to it than this. We are ambivalent about scientific explanations. We want both to control and to feel that insoluble mysteries remain so that no one controls everything. Homoeopathy caters to both desires at once.

Its remedies are almost infinite dilutions of commonplace substances or botanical extracts, which makes their mode of action profoundly mysterious from a physiological point of view, overthrowing all the known laws of physics, chemistry and biology. As nine out of ten maladies get better by themselves (a fact denied by homoeopathists), this gives any kind of therapy, medical or otherwise, a great head start. If, in addition, such treatment causes no side-effects, its fortune is made.

The fact, incidentally, that most maladies cure themselves, and that this is important for establishing the efficacy of treatment, has been known for a long time. Take only one example, that of Gideon Harvey (no relation of William). In his *The Art of Curing Diseases by Expectation* of 1689, he wrote:

'If antiquity be capable of conferring validity, the art of

expectation being contemporary with that of physick, may be termed equally valuable. In many cases they are synonymous, where the cure is attributed to the art of medicine, which in reality was chiefly performed by the art of expectation; the remedies, that were the tools of the former, being of little or no efficacy, and consequently delusory; whereas time, delays, and doing nothing, are the principal media of the latter.'

This is a lesson no sooner taught than forgotten, like the elementary principle that correlation does not prove causation. Despite our best intentions, our psyche struggles with logic and frequently emerges the victor.

There is another practical advantage of homoeopathy. Not so many years ago, doctors were allowed to prescribe placebos knowingly. The father of a friend of mine, a general practitioner in a market town, used to keep three bottles of medicine which was, in fact, water. One was clear but slightly flavoured, another green, and a third red. If the clear liquid did not work, the patient graduated to the green, and finally to the red. Patients in the waiting room would discuss which stage they had reached, shaking their heads sadly over those who had reached the red, which was known to be reserved for only the most serious cases.

It goes almost without saying that such a manner of proceeding is completely forbidden nowadays. It would be regarded as fraud. When a modern doctor wishes to take advantage of the placebo effect, paradoxically, he is obliged to employ a real medication with real physiological effects, which introduces the possibility of real, unpleasant and harmful side-effects. Doctors therefore prescribe remedies which just might have a therapeutic effect, the diagnosis never being a hundred per cent certain.

And from this it is just a short and tempting step for the doctor to believe that, when the patient gets better, he has done so because of the prescription. In other words, instead of deceiving the patient, the doctor now deceives both the patient and himself. The gross overmedication of the population is but a different branch of the same tree.

It now falls to me to relate my late mother's encounter with homoeopathy in her eightieth year. She developed a rash on her scalp so severe that her hair began to fall out. For anyone this would be alarming and upsetting, but my mother had made her personal appearance an important focus of her life, and a matter of great pride. She tried to see a dermatologist on the National Health Service, but, her condition not being life-threatening, she was informed that she would have to wait for some months. She didn't want to wait and resorted to two dermatologists in private practice. The first prescribed for her an application to the scalp that made her condition very much worse. Indeed, it disfigured her so badly that she was reluctant to go out. She then sought the opinion of another dermatologist whose efforts were, if anything, even more disastrous. Finally, she turned to the Royal Homoeopathic Hospital, as it was then still called (it is now the Royal London Hospital for Integrated Medicine, a weaselly name if ever there was one). There she was prescribed little silvery pills containing an infinitesimal dose of *echinacea angustifolia*, the purple cone-flower, that looked as if they had been made in artisanal fashion. No sooner did she begin to take them than her condition improved, and before long she was cured.

What were the theoretical implications of her case? She had developed a serious rash spontaneously, without obvious cause. She had tried the treatment of two specialist dermatologists and it had made her condition far worse. After many weeks she consulted a homoeopath and was given effectively a placebo and the condition disappeared.

Of course, for my mother the general lesson to be drawn, if there was one, was of no importance by comparison with the disappearance of her condition. It would have been difficult to persuade her that it was not the homoeopathist's silvery pills that had cured her. I also knew that my mother delighted in symptoms that baffled her doctor—the better to conceal her true diagnosis. Nor did the failure of medical science (referred to by homoeopaths as 'allopathy') in this case deter her in the slightest from consulting her GP on numerous subsequent occasions for other matters.

A doctor treats the individual and not whole classes of individuals, and inexplicable individual responses to medication are commonplace. I once had a patient in Africa who suffered from cerebral malaria and who continued in a confused state several days after the malaria had been cured. As it happened, I had just read a paper in a medical journal establishing (by means of a controlled trial) the uselessness of steroids in the treatment of cerebral malaria. But in this case, rather than sit by helplessly and watch my patient dwindle by inanition, I decided to try them on the general grounds that there was probably inflammation of his brain (which steroids might reduce). His recovery was remarkable and in two days he was perfectly fit.

Needless to say, I attributed his recovery to my treatment and not to a placebo effect of the steroids—the latter very unlikely in such a case. A controlled trial may conceal within its large groups small subgroups to whom the general conclusions of the trial do not apply. At any rate, that is what I told myself. But what is sauce for the goose is sauce for the gander; and the homoeopath who treated my mother might have thought the same for himself her case.

At least I was aware of this problem, which poor Dr Clarke—admittedly like most physicians of his time—was not. As far as I can tell, he spent a large part of his life (1853-1931) issuing unmediated statements and attacking others practitioners, even of homoeopathy, as ignorant. There is no disputing his industry, to judge by the number of books he wrote, some of them still in print. He had a very large fashionable practice, in his early days making house-calls in a carriage specially fitted with a writing-desk so that he should waste no time between them. He was for many years editor of *The Homoeopathic World*, and the only picture of him that I have been able to find shows a distinguished-looking man with white hair, elegantly dressed. In homoeopathic circles he is regarded as a classic author who introduced new regimens into homoeopathic practice and trained non-medical people in its ideas, including his successor at *The Homoeopathic World*, the economist and historian, J. Ellis Barker.

The obituary in Clarke's own journal admitted that, because of his early struggles, he was impatient of those who opposed him or his views, but ended: 'Our enmities die, our friendships live for ever.' Whether or not this is true, Dr Clarke was certainly a good hater. His earliest enmity expressed in print was towards our old friend vivisection. But Dr Clarke, friend of the animals, was no pacifist and during the slaughter of the Great War, he turned his attention to greater enemies than the vivisectionists—the Germans and the Jews.

In his pamphlet of 1917 titled 'The Sword', he writes that, 'Hebrews all over the world have an open or concealed affection for the cause of the German [Kaiser] and the Turk [Ataturk].' Another passage runs, 'Shylock has no part in the blood of England.'

His next non-medical literary production, in 1919, was to edit and write a preface for *England under the Heel of the Jew* and another of his pamphlets was 'White Labour: or the Jew in International Politics'. But his main anti-Semitic work was in editing and contributing to journals such as the *Jew Ueber Alles*, later renamed *The Hidden Hand*. From 1920 until his death in 1931 he was the chairman of The Britons, a groupuscule whose main aim was in fact compulsory Zionism, forcing all British Jews to emigrate to Palestine. Physical extermination was not a viable alternative for the publication Clarke edited. Not because it was morally wrong, but because the kind-hearted British would not like it. The Britons, never a very large political formation, became in time mainly a publishing venture, the Britons Publishing Society—later Company—and was responsible for the publication of many editions of the anti-Semitic historical hoax, *Protocols of the Elders of Zion*, that was first published in Russia.

As mentioned, Dr Clarke's main friend, disciple, and later continuator at the *Homoeopathic World* (which he soon renamed *Heal Yourself* and turned into a mass-market publication), was J. Ellis Barker. Curiously enough, he was born Julius Otto Eltzbacher and the son of a Jewish doctor in Cologne. He came to England before the Great War, where he tried in book after book to warn Brits against the German threat, and changed his name to Barker during the war because of anti-German feeling. While he had no medical qualifications towards the end of his life (he died in 1948 at the age of seventy eight) he wrote successful books with titles such as *The Miracle of Healing*. It is said that Barker hid or disguised his Jewish origins, which perhaps explains why Dr Clarke accepted him as friend and disciple. But Barker had been involved in a high-profile libel case in which his family background had been brought up, and no less a figure than Winston Churchill had made public reference to them.

The veneration of the Romanian physiologist and professor of medicine, Nicolae Paulescu, suffers from a similar ambiguity as Dr Clarke's. As a scientist, Paulescu's achievements were of an altogether different calibre from Clarke's placebos. He is held by some to have been the true discoverer of insulin and unjustly passed over for the Nobel Prize which was instead awarded to Banting and Best. They admitted more than forty years later that they had misinterpreted his paper announcing his discovery because it was written in French, of which they did not have a good command.

Paulescu was also politically active as a vehement anti-Semite. He wrote a book suggesting genocide as the 'solution' in a country where pogroms and actual violence against Jewish citizens were commonplace. He died in the same year as Clarke, before the worst excesses were committed in Romania (which were unspeakably bad), however, and by all accounts he was sensitive and kindly. A Jewish doctor who trained under him at the University of Bucharest defended his memory—as a scientist.

It seems to me that a person's opinions are more important to us now in assessing their character, and their actual conduct less important, than would once have been the case. Nowadays, Paulescu would be taken as a moral monster (as would Dr Clarke), and excluded from polite society irrespective of—in his case—Paulescu's other accomplishments. How opinion cancels anything else is shown by the reaction to a few words (light-hearted and taken out of context) by professor Sir Timothy Hunt, a Nobel Prize-winning scientist, and an otherwise mild-mannered man.

When, in the last days of the Ceausescu regime, I visited Paulescu's grave, there was a single red rose placed across it. Was it there to commemorate the physiologist or the anti-Semite?

17

Siren Questions
Delia Bacon

The attractions of conspiracy theories are great—paranoia is never far below the surface of our minds and can be provoked by many slight physiological derangements, besides being the permanent condition of many. In the section of the Brecon bookshop devoted to literary biography, history and criticism, I found two books devoted to the most amusing of conspiracy theories concerning the authorship of Shakespeare. They were *Lord Oxford Was Shakespeare* by Lt-Col. Montagu W. Douglas, published in 1934, and *The Shakespeare Claimants* by H.N. Gibson, published in 1962.

The whole controversy was started by an American woman of unstable mentality called Delia Bacon. It was she who first gave currency to the idea that the principal author of the plays was not Shakespeare, the boy from Stratford, but Francis Bacon, who used the name of Shakespeare as a front—in her opinion. In 1857 she published her unreadable *magnum opus, The Philosophy of the Plays of Shakespeare Unfolded*, with a preface by Nathaniel Hawthorne, then American consul in Liverpool. He, however, wrote it out of kindness to her and did not actively endorse her theory, an implied disavowal that earned him her undying enmity. She had by then spent several years in Stratford, pondering Shakespeare's plays and communing with the spirit of the place. She convinced herself that Bacon had interred documents relating to his authorship of the plays in Shakespeare's tomb, and almost got the vicar to believe it too.

But before she could have the slab to the tomb lifted she was interned in a local private asylum, from which she returned to America, where she spent the last years of her life in the Retreat, the famous asylum of Hartford, Connecticut, where she died. It is unclear whether she developed the theory because she was mad, was driven mad by her theory, or had some other condition incidental to her theory. Nonetheless, her nephew, Theodore Bacon, wrote a memoir of his aunt which began: 'This is the story of a life that was neither splendid in achievement nor adventure, nor successful, nor happy. It began in a New World wilderness, in the simplicity of a refined and honest poverty; it continued for almost fifty years of labour and sorrow, and ended amid clouds of disappointment and distraction.'[1]

One cannot help but sympathise with such a life, but when Theodore Bacon claims no 'splendid' achievement on behalf of his aunt he underestimates her true impact on the world. Though her book was received with derision, it launched not a thousand ships but an Armada of books concerning the 'true' authorship of Shakespeare—that is to say, William Shakespeare of Stratford-upon-Avon, hitherto considered the sole author of his works.

The theory that Shakespeare was not Shakespeare spread like wildfire and attracted many eminent persons, among them Henry James, Mark Twain, and Sigmund Freud. This in itself is remarkable and one may wonder why it attracted people of such calibre. I suspect that it was for the same reason that Tolstoy hated, and George Bernard Shaw denigrated, Shakespeare.[2] His genius by means of which he is able to describe a vast range of humans, and to make us feel that we know what it is like actually to be them, and moreover to convey this in language of unrivalled beauty, is unique in history. To question the authorship, in the knowledge that once raised the question will never be answered to universal satisfaction, is to diminish Shakespeare a little.[3]

The books on 'the authorship question' give me another kind of pleasure, amounting almost to relief, such that, if I had my life again, I might consider a career as a scholar of the question.

What I like most about Delia Bacon's theory is that it is inexhaustible and quite without practical importance. It can arouse great passion, permitting vituperation without murderous hatred, and satisfy the inner pedant that is present in so many of us.[4] One of my Baconian books, *The Bacon-Shakespeare Anatomy* (1944), by W.S. Melsome, a consulting surgeon and also author of *The Value of Bacteriological Examination before, during and after Surgical Operations* (1898)—the Shakespeare-manuscript delivered to the publisher a few days before Melsome's death. While he was writing it, the Second World War must have seemed far away, a mere buzzing in the background. Melsome, in his middle to late seventies as he wrote, at least had no need of tedious journeys to libraries, for, according to the preface of his book, he had acquired such a prodigious knowledge of and memory for the works of Bacon and Shakespeare (one and the same person in his view), that he was able to collate hundreds of similar passages from them simply from the depths of his own brain.

Lt-Col. Douglas, the author of my new purchase, was not a Baconian, he was an Oxfordian. For over sixty years after the publication of Delia Bacon's book the Baconians had it almost all their own way in the market for finding the real author of Shakespeare, but in 1920 a schoolmaster with a name which his publisher begged him, unsuccessfully, not to use, J. Thomas Looney, published his *Shakespeare Identified in Edward De Vere, the Seventeenth Earl of Oxford*. It was a book which not only started a flood of Oxfordianism (Freud was a convert) but encouraged others to propose their own candidates, of whom there are now well in excess of fifty.[5] In this sense, Shakespeare has much in common with Jack the Ripper.

Douglas was a humble follower and continuator of Looney, but he was not therefore an inconsiderable man. He was an administrator in British India who, in 1897, investigated an allegation of conspiracy to murder brought against the founder of the Muslim Ahmadiyya sect, Mirza Ghulam Ahmad, who believed (and persuaded many others to believe) that he was the Messiah sent to bring final peace to the world by converting it entirely to Islam.[6] Douglas, then of the rank of captain, dismissed the charges, earning the praise of Ahmad in his subsequent, highly diffuse, book on the case. If Colonel Douglas did not believe in the conspiracy to murder, he certainly believed in the conspiracy to conceal the identity of the author of the plays and poems attributed to William Shakespeare. He took the view that Oxford was only one of a group of aristocrats who wrote the plays, even if he were by far the most productive and significant of them.

When you enter, or stumble into, a labyrinthine controversy like that of the true authorship of Shakespeare, you tend to be at the mercy of the last book that you read. Personally I am by inclination a Stratfordian, as the Baconians, Oxfordians and others call those who cleave to the traditional view ('Stratfordian' always carrying a slight tone of disparagement, as if to believe in Shakespeare, the boy from Stratford, as Shakespeare, the author of the plays, was akin to believing in the flatness of the earth).[7] I have yet to read anything on the subject that has compelled me to change my mind.

In a tribute to the theories pivoting on class, legal knowledge, education etc., I once argued that Shakespeare must have been a doctor, so accurate were many of his clinical observations, only to then turn this hypothesis on its head to prove that he could not possibly have been a doctor, for his clinical observations were far too accurate for him to have received the medical education of his time. You only have to compare *Select Observations on English Bodies* by his son-in-law, Dr John Hall, who was indeed a doctor of medicine, with Shakespeare's own observations, to realise that education can be blind as well as illuminating. Dr Hall was the victim of the medical doctrine of his day, a lens so distorting that he saw nothing through it and that his therapeutic principle seemed to be making treatment so unpleasant that the patient would get better from fear of it, or at least stop complaining about the ailment, it being the lesser of two evils.[8]

Somewhat to my surprise, *The Shakespeare Claimants* by H.N. Gibson was the best book on the subject that I had ever read, clearly argued and elegantly written. Claiming at the outset to have no axe to grind ('I may add that I began my research as a Shakespearean agnostic')—but who would start a book of this nature by declaring a strong prejudice?—he makes short shrift of most of the arguments employed by the various -ians and -ites. 'It was only when I began a detailed examination of the various theories that I discovered how really weak and unconvincing these were, and when brought together and compared, what a devastating wreck they made of one another.'

Gibson's most important argument seems to me not only those of a proper literary scholar, but also more or less conclusive.[9] The very plethora of candidates, at least two of them with as much evidence in their favour as the other, speaks against the anti-Stratfordian hypothesis. If the same kind of evidence is as much in favour of Oxford as of Bacon, that kind of evidence cannot be of much evidential value. If you are going to argue that Shakespeare (the boy from Stratford) couldn't have written the plays because he left no books in his will, you should at least know what the wills of other playwrights of the period contained; and if, likewise, you argue that there are parallels between x's work and y's, and that this demonstrates that x is really y, you should at least know whether there are equal parallels with the works of u, v, w and z. To anyone not blinded by his darling theory, this might seem blindingly obvious, but it never seemed to occur to the anti-Stratfordians. There have been some Baconians who have gone so far as to claim that Bacon wrote not only the works of Shakespeare, but those of every other Elizabethan playwright, as well as the works of Sir Philip Sydney, Robert Burton's *The Anatomy of Melancholy*, the authorised version of the bible, and Montaigne's *Essays*.

Who then was H.N. Gibson? The cover-flap of the book is completely silent on this matter. The title page says he is M.A., Ph.D., but that is all. There is a slight clue as to his career when, in the introduction he says, 'It has been my business for many years to lecture on Shakespeare to senior forms in schools and to adults in W.E.A. [Workers' Educational Association] classes'. We might conclude that he had never attained the higher reaches of academia, but just as not every slippery slope is slid down so not every career ladder is ambitiously climbed. Other than the fact that his wife was called Winifred, a name hardly given, to whom he dedicated his book, there is no biography—which is in itself a fact of interest. The book is like an anonymous message in a bottle thrown into the great sea of literary studies.[10]

Of H.N. Gibson I have since managed to find very little apart from the fact that H.N. stands for Harry Norman. There is a Winifred Gibson who published books up to fourteen years before the publication of *The Shakespeare Claimants*, with titles such as *The Right Way to Swim*, *Swimming for Schools* and *The Shallow Water Method of Swimming*, which one bookseller described rather cruelly as

'Quite the funniest and silliest instruction manual I have ever seen.' I wonder whether she was H.N.'s wife, for she must have been a schoolteacher, too. H.N. Gibson was also the co-author, with Freda M(argaret) Kelsall, of a convoluted comic novel, *Double, Double*, published in 1965 (and never since), satirising the whole authorship question, in which it is suggested by characters in the book that William Shakespeare was actually a pair of identical twins separated at birth, one of whom remained behind in Stratford, the other going off to London to be an actor, his lines provided by his stay-at-home genius of a brother, who was also a local businessman dealing in various commodities.

This theory is also plausible, except for one small historical detail that ruins it entirely. The father of Shakespeare's London associate from Stratford, Richard Quiney, wrote to his son suggesting that he tell Shakespeare that 'knit stockings were selling profitably in Evesham market' with a view to involving him in the trade. Thus, Shakespeare the playwright and Shakespeare the merchant were one and the same person (assuming, evidently, that Shakespeare was, in fact, the author). The point of all this is to demonstrate how easily a theory may be construed and remain plausible in the absence of a fly-in-the-ointment document whose survival or disappearance is largely a matter of chance.

Practically none of the anti-Stratfordians are either Shakespearian scholars or scholars of the Elizabethan period but rather retired admirals, colonels, judges, civil servants, doctors, research chemists, insurance brokers, astrophysicists, organists, and so forth, who take up the question comparatively late in life in what one suspects is an obsessive quest for meaning and purpose. My favourite is Dr Orville Ward Owen (1854-1924), physician of Detroit. He was a successful doctor who, for relaxation from his busy practice, committed the whole of Shakespeare to memory. Gradually he persuaded himself that the plays contained a hidden cipher establishing that Francis Bacon was their true author, and he constructed a complex machine to discover the hidden messages.

The *New York Times* of 14 May, 1911, describes Dr Owen's manner of proceeding. 'It [the key to the cipher] is taken from the third supplement of Philip Sydney's "Arcadia".'

Starting with the word 'Bacon' in mind, Dr Owen begins with the first line of the supplement commencing with the letter 'B', and goes on to the end of the sentence. Then he turns to the end of the supplement, and takes the first line commencing with 'A', continuing to the end of the sentence. Then back again to the beginning of the supplement for the first line commencing with 'C', and so on, alternating until the supplement is exhausted and dozens of sentences beginning B A C O N is the result. This is only the beginning:

'Having done this he makes use of a spider's web, mention of which is made in the preface to "Arcadia", and by ingeniously drawing light lines through all the letters "I" and "Y" appearing on the sheet, he finds that the lines all led to one centre, giving the sheet the appearance of a spider's web, while in the centre itself appear these letters:

HID
UN
DER
WYE

Given the convoluted method, it is not altogether surprising, perhaps, that Dr Owen's *magnum opus*, titled *Sir Francis Bacon's Cipher Story*, was five volumes long, or that he found other messages, too, by means of circles drawn at various points on the sheet mentioned above, such as 'Bed of braced beams under Roman ford.'

Putting two and two together to make about eight hundred million, he concluded that Bacon-Shakespearian secrets lay buried in the mud at the bottom of the river Wye in Chepstow, which he determined to dig up with mechanical dredgers.[11] He had to obtain permission both from the government and the Duke of Beaufort, who had what sounds like the feudal rights to the flotsam and jetsam of the River Wye, and he managed so to persuade the Duke of the reality of his speculations that the Duke paid many of the expenses of the whole proceedings.

Dr Owen (who also wrote two Shakespearian history plays, *The Historical Tragedy of May Queen of Scots* and *The Tragical History of Our Later Brother, the Earl of Essex*, both of which I have read remembering of them only that they were not of fully Shakespearian quality, to say the least) hired dredgers at £85 a day, the equivalent of something like £8000 in our money, to scour the Wye at Chepstow, where his wife and four children stayed for a year and a half while he carried out the work.[11] Eventually he uncovered a large wooden structure that everyone else, prosaically, believed was an old landing stage (especially as he found something similar on the other side of the river). But Dr Owen was confident that underneath it was buried the chest that would contain the secret of Bacon-Shakespeare. He found nothing further of the sort.

The writer of the article in the *New York Times* was unimpressed by Dr Owen's method, and wrote 'As I saw the cipher—a mass of letters from which it would be possible, one would imagine, with close application to form any sentence—it spoke volumes for the patience, enthusiasm, optimism, and earnestness which Dr Owen has devoted to his life's work.' Nonetheless, Dr Owen appeals to me because of his undoubted integrity, his Quixotic self-delusion, and most of all because he was a deeply tragic figure whose suffering (and the distress of his wife and children)[12] was the consequence of mirage, not of malice. His search under the Wye ruined him financially and he never recovered his medical practice. He died deeply impoverished and on his deathbed he said that he wished he had never come across the Baconian hypothesis.

I will mention something about my particular copy of *The Shakespeare Claimants*. It bears a single, neat but angled stamp, HAFOD-y-DDÔL SCHOOL LIBRARY. This was a grammar school in Nantyglo, a working-class industrial town in South Wales. The stamp, I think, is of almost the same age as the book and in those days, now as seemingly far off as those of Periclean Athens, intelligent children from poor homes were not assumed to be uninterested in matters far removed from their experience of daily life.[13] The teachers thought then—or rather took for granted—that the very purpose of education was to broaden and deepen as far as possible the child's notions of what was relevant to him or her, and even perhaps to suggest that there were some things worth studying for their own sake, for their intrinsic delight.

---

[1] *Distraction* here means madness.

[2] Nearly fifty-five years ago, under the influence of a schoolmaster who was a confirmed Shavian, I read Shaw's early novel, *An Unsocial Socialist*, of which, never having re-read it, I remember only one line, no doubt only approximately, which impressed me greatly at the time. A schoolgirl says, 'Shakespeare—silly old fool expects credit for saying things that everybody knows.'

[3] My copy of Sir Edwin Durning-Lawrence's *Bacon Is Shakespeare* (1912) once belonged to Sir Ernest Shackleton, the polar explorer, who may not have been a genius but was certainly very distinguished. Mere possession of the book does not prove him to have been a Baconian, of course, any more than it proves me to be a Baconian; but still I suspect that he was.

[4] In 1950, the BBC Third Programme broadcast a talk by the Curator of Rare Books at the Folger Shakespeare Library in Washington, Dr Giles F. Dawson, in which he dismissed anti-Stratfordian theories, of which at the time the Baconian was by far the most prominent (the torch having since been passed on to the Oxfordians). The Baconians demanded, but were not granted, the right of reply: as if the matter were one of a political election and the BBC were obliged by its charter to maintain a balance. We may be thankful that the controversy distracts so many distinguished minds from the much less interesting sphere of party politics.

[5] The authorship question is of interest even outside the English-speaking world. Recently I saw an article in *Le Monde* claiming that the Sonnets were written by John Florio. The sonnet was an Italian poetic form, Florio was the author of the first English-Italian dictionary, *ergo* etc.

[6] Bizarre as the beliefs of the sect may appear to those who do not share them, they are at least entirely peaceful and tolerant.

[7] Another candidate for the true authorship of Shakespeare is William Stanley, fifth Earl of Derby. Those who believe in him are known as Derbyites, a term that (in my ear at least) carries with it its own disparagement. Perhaps this is because I knew a bookseller who was also a firm believer in the Albanian school of communism and who called all traitors to the left-wing cause -ites of one kind or another: for example, supporters of the British Labour

Party were the Labourites, while worse still, far worse, were the Khrushchevites. By contrast, supporters of Christopher Marlowe as the author are the Marlovians, a term of no connoted disparagement. Enver Hoxha, incidentally, was an amusing writer by the standards of communist leaders, with an enviable line in vituperation.

8   The fact that Marlowe died in 1593 is not a problem for Marlovians. For them it was not Marlowe who was killed in the brawl in Deptford over a bill, but a stand-in. Marlowe was spirited abroad afterwards, living in Flanders, from the safety of which he sent the plays back to England.

9   Colonel Douglas, an eminent Oxfordian, is concerned only to refute the Stratfordians. The Baconians do not come into his line of fire at all, as if they hardly existed, though in fact Baconian literature, even at the time he wrote, would have filled a substantial library.

10   The cover of a slightly earlier book on the auctorial question, *Shakespeare and His Betters*, by R.C. Churchill, also has no biographical information about the author.

11   Dr Owen also interested himself in the technology of spiritualist levitation. Percy Allen, one of the most prominent and, if I may so put it, militant of the Oxfordians, communicated directly with reputed author by spiritualist means. The shade of Oxford avowed that he was indeed the author of the plays.

12   But, for all I know, Mrs Owen may have been the Mrs Micawber of the authorship question.

13   It is the glory, or rather one of the glories, of Shakespeare himself that he is never very far from the experience of our daily lives.

18

Coincidences
Oversmoking

Coincidence is the mother of many a conspiracy theory. There was a book next to the two Shakespeare authorship volumes about William Blake by Max Plowman, published in 1927. By coincidence Dr J.H. Clarke, the homoeopathist whose book on colds I had already selected for purchase, had also published a book on Blake in 1927. His was titled *William Blake on the Lord's Prayer*, while Plowman's was titled *An Introduction to the Study of Blake*.

Coincidence preys on the mind, despite the fact that a world without them would have to be a world that was very poor in events. The most striking coincidence in my life was a telephone call from someone I had lost contact with for fifteen years after having been friendly on the other side of the world for three or four. Seemingly out of the blue he rang and we said that we must meet after we both returned from a forthcoming trip abroad.

'Where are you going?' I asked.

'South America,' he replied.

'So am I. When are you going?'

'The day after tomorrow.'

'So am I. Which flight are you taking?'

'Avianca to Bogota.'

'So am I.'

Not to have been struck by this would have been impossible. Plowman and Clarke were both keen Blakeans, though it was not altogether a coincidence that they should have published their books about Blake in 1927, for that was the centenary of his death.

When it comes to Blake, I myself never get very far. By the time I come to read another book about him I have forgotten most of what I have read before. My problem is that Blake's work, except for the grandeur of the language, is laden with symbols that mean nothing much to me. Even once the meaning[1] of the symbols has been explained, I am too impatient to remember who, exactly, Los, Enitharmon, Urthona, Tharmas and Enion, etc. are.

Yet I am greatly moved by the *Songs of Innocence and of Experience* and the 'Auguries of Innocence'. Few men wrote so many simple and memorable, yet evocative, lines:

Little fly,
Thy summer's play
My thoughtless hand
Has brush'd away.

Am not I
A fly like thee?
Or art not thou
A man like me?

For I dance,
And drink, and sing,
Till some blind hand

Shall brush my wing.[2]

Both Plowman and Dr Clarke agreed with Blake that rules and prohibitions play no part in morality and that they are manifestations of life- and spirit-denying pharisaism. Clarke, in his book, returns to his obsession with anti-Semitism, and duly enrols Blake in the struggle against the influence of the Jews. Citing Heinrich Heine, 'Puritanism is only Judaism with the addition of a license to eat pork', Clarke argues, 'It is the deliverance of men's minds and souls from the blight of this puritan mentality which Blake felt himself inspired to effect.'

Plowman mentions Dr Clarke's book in a letter, writing that he had been told by an academic that 'in spite of its anti-Semite balderdash there was something in it.' Setting aside the balderdash, Clarke's book is an extended commentary on Blake's critical notes on Dr Thornton's new translation of the Lord's Prayer of 1827, which admittedly was almost as ghastly as many of the snivelling modern translations of the Bible—'Grant unto me, and the whole world, day by day, an abundant supply of spiritual and corporeal Food', instead of 'Give us this day our daily bread'. Blake's objection to Thornton's translation, nonetheless, was religio-ideological rather than aesthetic, and he attacked it as 'most malignant & artful'.

Poor Dr Robert John Thornton (1768-1837). Did he really deserve such a bilious charge? A physician, he wrote not only on medical subjects and translated Virgil (illustrated by Blake), but produced perhaps the most beautiful botanical book ever published in English, *The*

Temple of Flora. Its illustrations now sell for thousands each, the volumes having largely been broken up for the purposes of such sale, and a complete volume now costs hundreds of thousands. In the process of publishing this work, however, Dr Thornton, ruined himself financially and died in abject poverty.

Max Plowman (1883-1941) was a much more sympathetic character than Dr Clarke, the anti-Semitic homoeopath. He was a socialist and pacifist, his face, out-standingly craggy in middle age, seemingly with a nose of Cyrano de Bergerac proportions, and his eyes too far apart, his ears a little on the flappy side. He was certainly not an armchair idealist. Like Sir Edmund Gosse he was born into a family of Plymouth Brethren, a particularly severe sect of joyless puritans. He abandoned the sect and, like Gosse, made literature his lodestar. He joined up in 1914, initially as an ambulance-man in the hope of avoiding real violence. But as he felt that there was no middle course between proper fighting and complete pacifism, and arguing that he could not ask other men to do his fighting for him,[3] he took a commission in the infantry.

He was injured and suffered from shell-shock and was treated at Craiglockhart psychiatric hospital. Early in 1918 he resigned from his infantry commission by letter and narrowly missed imprisonment for refusal to return to the war as a conscript (the war came to an end before the mills could grind small enough). After the war, he devoted himself to agitating for pacifism, peacefully of course, the study of William Blake, writing a little deeply-felt, but not very good, poetry, and helping to run the *Adelphi* magazine,

which ran from 1923 to 1955 and, in his day, had very distinguished contributors including George Orwell. He also
wrote a memoir of his war experiences, *A Subaltern on the
Somme*, published under the pseudonym, Mark VII, in 1928.
Many of the best anti-war memoirs gestated for at least ten
years after the War's end before they were published, as if
raw memory had to pass through many filters before the
meaning of the experience could be fully apprehended.[4]

Plowman would hardly have approved of me. In a letter
to the novelist and belle-lettrist, Rayner Heppenstall, he
wrote: 'to be able to observe and recognise the feelings of
others with a pure objective recognition is to be of the
Devil.' This outlook, of course, is the aim of a doctor and
psychiatrist. Of psychiatry in general he wrote in the same
letter: 'Psychiatry is thus the XXth cent. witchcraft, & its
unmitigated practice the employment of demons.' This was
written in 1936, and prescient. Psychiatry has moved away
from the treatment of the obviously mad to claim
sovereignty over all forms of human distress and
misconduct. In the twenty-first century it does resemble
witchcraft, with its medications often (though not always)
serving as eye of newt and wool of bat.

There was another connection between Plowman and
Clarke that was pure coincidence. For many years,
Plowman suffered severely from peptic ulcer—as early as
1928. In 1941, three days before his death and in the last
letter he ever wrote, he said: 'I arise from the severest
torments of gastric ulcer (only as far as the pillows) to
scrawl these lines on paper, & for the past few days those
pains have been too severe to make writing of any sort

possible.' In the letters in 1927 he writes that he will have to go for an X-ray to the Homoeopathic Hospital, where Dr Clarke was a consultant.

Reading Plowman's account of his agonies discomfited me. My father suffered from the same condition for as long as did Plowman. I never made proper allowances for what he was suffering from, hastily ascribing his ulcer to his bad temper rather than his bad temper to his ulcer.[5] My father had two operations on his ulcer, and one nearly killed him, admittedly in part because he insisted on discharging himself from hospital before his surgeon thought it advisable. In those days a large proportion of abdominal surgery continued to be performed for the alleviation of peptic ulceration until the discovery by Barry Marshall and Robin Warren in the early 1980s that infection with *helicobacter pylori* was the main (though not the only) cause of such ulceration, whereupon the surgery became largely redundant.

By another coincidence, also printed in 1927 like Plowman's and Clarke's, one of the books in my possession is *Two Lectures on Gastric and Duodenal Ulcer: A Record of Ten Years' Experience* by Sir Berkeley Moynihan, the greatest British abdominal surgeon of his day.[6] Moynihan described precisely the treatment, both medical and surgical, that my father received. I even recognised the conflict and rivalry that he described between physicians and surgeons—a little like that between Sunni and Shia—as to who was better able to cure the disease. Physicians said the surgeons killed their patients by operating on them, the surgeons said the physicians killed their patients by leaving them open to fatal perforations of their ulcers.[7] Patients themselves thus had the choice between being actively or passively killed.

Moynihan was clear that one of the causes of relapse after apparent cure of an ulcer was smoking; 'An "attack" of duodenal ulcer often follows an orgy of tobacco.' This was something my father, and Max Plowman (if he was ever told it), refused to believe. In my father's case it was because he didn't want to, or rather, he wanted both to be cured of his ulcer and, contrary to the advice of doctors, continue to smoke his terrible pipe. He disliked intensely any condition of subordination to others, including (or especially) those better informed on a subject than he.

I doubt from what I have read of him that Plowman was of the same ilk. In his day it was assumed that a man would smoke—only the Nazis were really opposed to it. Even Sir Berkeley Moynihan was not really against smoking and warned, not against it, but against what he called 'oversmoking'.

---

[1] Or supposed meaning, since everyone interprets them differently.

[2] As flies to wanton boys are we to th' gods,
They kill us for their sport.

                                    King Lear, Act IV, scene 1

[3] One of my objections to the death penalty is that I would not be prepared myself to participate in it—for ethical and not merely aesthetic reasons. Could I properly ask others to do what I consider unethical to do myself?

[4] Edmund Blunden's *Undertones of War* was published in 1928; Robert Graves's *Goodbye to All That* was published in 1929; Siegfried Sassoon's *Memoirs of an Infantry Officer* was published in 1930. Erich Maria Remarque's novel, *All Quiet on the Western Front*, was published in 1929.

[5] It goes without saying that the effect of physical suffering on conduct must pass through character and temperament. Max Plowman was by all accounts a good-tempered man.

6   It is strange how many of the great men of British medicine of that era had names that seemed to destine their bearers for distinction: Arbuthnot Lane, Farquhar Buzzard, and so forth. With names such as those, you could hardly become a postman or a ticket inspector. Two of the greatest British neurologists, the second of whom was in more or less apostolic succession to the first, were Henry Head and W. Russell Brain.

7   One of Moynihan's arguments in favour if surgery, at least in gastric ulceration, was that it extirpated the ulcer and thereby the risk of malignancy developing from that ulcer. But achlorhydria, the failure of the stomach to produce hydrochloric acid in normal quantities, is associated with cancer of the stomach. My father had an operation (vagotomy) that reduced his production of hydrochloric acid. Just over thirty years later, he died of the stomach cancer that he had long worried about developing.

19

Metaphysics
More Moral Children

When I was a young man I thought that metaphysics and epistemology were important. It stood to reason, or so it seemed to me, that one could not know anything until one knew what it was to know something. I now realise (and I think a still small voice, which I ignored, told me so at the time) that this was actually an excuse for mental laziness, for not learning more than the minimum necessary to pass exams. Endless speculation about intangibles was easy and painless; the slow accumulation of information was difficult and painful. I was helped in this realisation by an acquaintance of mine who claimed that he was going to reform and refound the basis of all human knowledge, which even I could see was a ridiculous ambition. If my acquaintance has since succeeded in his efforts, the world has not yet taken cognisance of the fact.

For years I did not pick up a book of philosophy. But now I am slightly drawn to them again, especially if they are short. On the shelves in the bookshop in Brecon, beside Max Plowman, I spied a slim volume titled *Reason and Morals* by John Wilson, published in 1961, that is to say a few years before the age of sexual intercourse began. The first two sentences, under the heading 'What Philosophers Do', read:

'The positivist movement in philosophy has now had thirty years in which to develop, expand and recapitulate. Philosophers who have been influenced by this movement are now not only regarded as intellectually and socially respectable, at least in academic and highbrow circles, but may even be said to exercise a dominant influence in many parts of the world.'[1]

The kind of positivism to which Wilson refers now seems appallingly thin as a doctrine. In its most extreme form, namely that a statement has meaning only if it is either empirically verifiable or tautologous (true by definition), it is itself meaningless by its own criteria, since it is neither provable empirically nor true by definition. Even if it were true by definition, it would tell us nothing of any importance. That positivists should have wanted to be socially-acceptable tells us something of the change that has overcome our society. Few nowadays desires to be respectable. On the contrary: in an age of mass bohemianism, the ground-zero is to be as unrespectable as possible.

John Wilson was a philosopher who seemed to belong to the long line of philosophers who think that, once we have got a grip on ourselves and our thoughts, no puzzles about human existence will remain. The philosopher will dissolve them as the sun dissolves morning mists: 'Conceptual ill-health, like emotional maladjustment, consists in the misuse, or misplacement, or misunderstanding of concepts and feelings. They must be put into proportion, saved from neurotic conflict with each other, reshaped and dovetailed.'

I happened to read a large part of Wilson's slim book (187 pages) while travelling on the Paris *métro* just before Christmas 2015, going between exhibitions and my wife's family. The *métro* was still almost deserted after the Bataclan terrorist attacks of November 13, and the city comparatively subdued.[2] Somehow, the notion of philosophical analysis as the answer to the terrorists' misplacement of concepts seemed shallow, the idea of someone who had led an existence sheltered from the world's evil. Though I did not doubt that they, the terrorists, were in some sense neurotic. Throughout the book, incidentally, the author showed a touching faith in the ability of psychoanalysis to resolve psychological problems, as if it were a science.

Wilson, who died in 2003, was mainly a philosopher of education. Like any good metaphysician would be, he was obsessed by the question of what education was for. In Britain nowadays, this is mainly so that mothers can go to work for low pay and that the youth-unemployment figures can be kept low, with the additional advantage of making the young pay for their own unemployment. I found the following in his obituary in the *Oxford Review of Education*: 'I first met John Wilson at Lincoln College in the mid-1960s… John was sorting out what needed to be done to make children more moral.'

It is difficult to know whether this was meant seriously or whether it was meant as satire. Does one make children moral, *à la* Gradgrind, or as one makes a plasticine model? Does one beat, exhort or exemplify children into morality? The obituary goes on to say: 'John typically saw that no progress could be made without agreement on what it means to be "moral", and that was a philosophical job.' Children will not be good, or at least better, until their elders have worked out what it means, metaphysically, to be good in other words. The history of philosophy—which has not completed the 'philosophical job' in more than two and a half millennia of trying—suggests that we may be waiting some time.

This reminded me of a few years earlier when I shared a platform in Adelaide with Germaine Greer on the subject of what it took to be good. Ms Greer said in her opening remarks that it required intelligence, to which I objected strongly, all the more so as she obviously regarded as intelligent only people as intelligent as she (in the same way that people think the rich are those who have more money than they). And since only one per cent of the population, about, was as intelligent as she, this meant that ninety-nine per cent of the population could not be good. Ms Greer denied that she had said any such thing, but people in the audience cried, 'Yes, you did.'

Wilson wrote the book on the cusp of a cultural change, indeed in a very tiny way may have contributed to it. He appears to have thought that 'our vices are no longer describable by their old names, but by words such as 'obsession', 'megalomania', 'complex', 'fixation' and so forth. He assumes in the book that this is a genuine advance in understanding, though in fact it is merely a change in nomenclature and connotation.

At the end of Wilson's book I had no clearer idea of the metaphysics of morals than I had at the beginning. I was also neither a better nor a worse person. I could not help but think of Hume's famous words:

'If we take in our hand any volume; of divinity or school metaphysics for instance; let us ask, Does it contain any abstract reasoning concerning quantity or number? No. Does it contain any experimental reasoning concerning matter of fact and existence? No. Commit it then to the flames: for it can contain nothing but sophistry and illusion.

[1]   Sir Alfred Ayer, the doyen of the English logical positivists, was only outwardly respectable. But then sensible upholders of respectability (in the Wilsonian sense) have always known that respectability was, and ought to be, an outward more than an inward quality.

[2]   Taxi drivers, those most important informants of foreign correspondents, told us that their takings were much reduced by comparison with normal.

20

Genius
The Indoor Aquarium

It is seventy miles through beautiful countryside from Brecon to Tenby, a walled town now subsisting (largely) on the sales of candy-floss to summer visitors. It is an elegant town, though the prospect of the eighteenth- and early-nineteenth-century terraces on the cliff-tops has been ruined by a large block of post-war flats, cunningly placed so that the eye cannot evade them however hard it tries. It is as if twentieth-century British architects, angered and frustrated by their own inability to create anything of value, have wreaked their revenge upon their predecessors. There is hardly a townscape in the land that has not suffered from the same spoliation.

It was off-season and we found a seaside guesthouse that, but for us, was empty. The owner, now in his late sixties, spoke with a pronounced Welsh accent, but his father had been an Italian prisoner of war who settled in Wales after being freed. He was obviously chatty by nature and was pleased to have someone to talk to. What he said was instructive. He divided humanity, or that part of it that comprised of summer coach parties from Lancashire and the Midlands, into three: a third would swallow hook line and sinker his outrageous fictional local history that he recounted to them over breakfast, a third would simply ignore it and get on with eating their eggs and bacon, and a third would laugh but not otherwise react. I suppose that is how voters divide in a parliamentary democracy.

For me the literary spirit of Tenby is Philip Henry Gosse. His *Tenby: A Sea-Side Holiday* was published in 1856—someone took my copy to the town in 1878—and is a series of letters to a friend about the marine life he found in the pools in the coves and islands of the coast near the town.

Gosse was brilliant, gifted, foolish, and almost tragic. He is mostly remembered as the father in Edmund Gosse's memoir *Father and Son*, published anonymously in 1907 (Henry James said that the son had 'a genius for inaccuracy'). A member of the Plymouth Brethren, P.H. Gosse was the inventor of the indoor aquarium and wrote many books popularising the study of natural history as an aid to piety, claiming that the seemingly miraculous contrivances of marine animals were proof of the power and wisdom of God.

He was also a talented artist and many of his books, not least *Tenby* among them, have beautiful coloured plates drawn by him, in which the love of and tenderness towards the creatures he draws is unmistakable. He feels for the individuals of the species that he describes: 'I poked my head into a dark hole, there basked the finest *bunodes crassicornis* that I had ever seen. He was indeed a magnificent fellow, and fully blown, with his thick tentacles distended to their utmost, and their beautiful tints softened and blended with the pellucid parts in the most charming manner.' Gosse is still a cited authority on this sea anemone, now classified as *urticina felina*, which has been known to live at least fifty years in an aquarium.

That Gosse regarded natural history as the continuation of religious worship by other means is obvious from his writing; and his illustrations of translucent invertebrate marine organisms of the most delicate anatomy and shades of colour are as much religious in inspiration as those, say, of Fra Angelico. Yet, as his *Tenby* demonstrates, he had a great respect for Darwin the naturalist. But he was a creationist who opposed the growing evidence in favour of evolution, and two years before Darwin published *On the Origin of Species* in 1859, Gosse published his own attempt to reconcile the geological record with the biblical story, literally interpreted, in *Omphalos* (navel), in which he alleges that all creatures were formed with the evidence of evolution within them, and the rocks fashioned with fossils.

In Tenby there is another institution that fills my heart with joy. It is a tiny shop on the corner of some steps that lead down to the sea. Inside, in one corner, which serves as his office and headquarters, sits the owner, the monarch of the little kingdom that he surveys. The rest of the establishment is given over to books.

At first sight the books appear to have slipped down a mountainside in an avalanche, as if a library atop a mountain had collapsed and its contents had tumbled downwards, coming to a halt in this tiny space. They are piled, or have come to rest, in such a way that if you hazard removing a book at the bottom or even in the middle of the pile, you risk of restarting the avalanche, in which case you might yourself be buried. Your room for manoeuvre in

the shop is very limited: at best you slide or tunnel your way
through the books. Astonishingly, the titles are in fact in
some kind of vague order—history, Welsh interest, sport,
drama, novels, transport. It is as unexpected in its way as
would be the proverbial monkey at the typewriter writing
Shakespeare.

What is so delightful about the owner is that he seems
to have no awareness whatever of how odd it all is. To the
genuine eccentric, of course, their eccentricity is the most
normal thing in the world. They are not trying to create an
impression, but merely doing things in the way that seems
natural to them.

This shop cannot be in a large way of business. The
only other person I have ever seen enter it called in for a
chat with the owner, and indeed four people in the shop
would be more crowded than one hundred thousand
people in a stadium seating fifty thousand. Yet it has
survived several years, and it reassures me that all is not yet
quite lost, that our freedom to do as we wish, to ignore for
example the rules relating to health and safety (surely the
dust from the books must give rise to occupational lung
disease?) has not quite been extinguished yet.

The last time I visited I bought a volume of Arthur
Wing Pinero's plays inscribed by the author. Pinero once
bestrode the world of the British stage like a colossus but
is now largely forgotten. He started out as a journeyman
actor and the *Dictionary of National Biography* cites a critic in
Birmingham of Pinero's Claudius in Hamlet that it was the
worst the city had ever seen. That instantly created a warm
place in my heart for him.[1]

I resisted the temptation to buy an inscribed first edition of Dylan Thomas's *Twenty-Five Poems* (his second book). It was £100 but my wife was with me and I did not want her to see with how little thought I was prepared to pay such a sum on a slim volume. I settled instead on the *Dr Thorndyke Omnibus* by R. Austin Freeman.

I bought it because the author, like his hero Thorndyke, was a doctor, and it was a way to show solidarity. I was attracted by the fine quality of its paper and excellent print, and by the fact that it had the rather beautiful bookplate of Sir John Ballinger (1860-1933), chief librarian of the National Library of Wales. He was a distinguished bibliographer as well as librarian, but not, apparently, altogether a nice man. The *Dictionary of National Biography* says of him that, 'in private an autocrat, he was popular with the public'. The *DNB* is relentless: Ballinger's 'lack of humour and austere sense of mission alienated many of his associates and he intimidated his subordinates.' The closer-up to him you got, it seems, the nastier he was. But he believed in public libraries, so he was not all bad.[2] Second was the matter of value for money. The book was marked at £3.[3] And finally there was the fact that Freeman, who derived much from his fellow-doctor Arthur Conan-Doyle, was the inventor of the inverted detective story, in which the criminal or perpetrator is known from the outset, and the mystery consists of the means in which he is detected.

If you wish to know the difference between industry on the one hand and genius on the other, that between Richard Austin Freeman and Arthur Conan Doyle will demonstrate it.

The parallels between the two men's lives are striking. They were born in 1862 and 1859 respectively; they both qualified as doctors, and both practised medicine for a time on the coast of England, Conan Doyle in Southsea and Austin Freeman in Gravesend; they both travelled to exotic destinations in their early adulthood (they were a few years apart in West Africa); they both wanted to be taken more seriously for their non-detective writing than that in the genre that made them famous (or rather, in the case of Austin Freeman, well-known). And the parallels between their protagonists in detection were even more striking. Both Sherlock Holmes and Dr John Thorndyke had medical companions to accompany them in their adventures and to record them as amanuenses, Dr Watson and Dr Jervis respectively. Although both Watson and Jervis were technically married, they might as well not have been, for they spent more time in the bachelor apartments of Holmes and Thorndyke than at home—the latter two had an absorbing interest in the arcana of human detritus, Holmes in cigar ash and Thorndyke in the various forms of household dust.

Indeed, one suspects Freeman of having copied Doyle. Although they were born only three years apart, Holmes appeared more than a decade and a half before Thorndyke. Austin Freeman was probably more deeply influenced by the Holmes stories than he thought he was. Conan Doyle's prose and dialogue flies off the page and sticks indelibly in the mind; Austin Freeman's remains page-bound. Freeman, apparently, was of the opinion that a detective story was predominantly an intellectual puzzle; Conan Doyle believed, or made, it a comedy of manners. Nowhere is the difference between the two writers more evident than in their dialogue.

Here, taken at random, is the beginning of a story called *The Contents of a Mare's Nest* by Freeman

'It is very unsatisfactory,' said Mr Stalker, of the Griffin Life Assurance Company, at the close of a consultation of on a doubtful claim.

'I suppose we shall have to pay up.'

'I am sure you will,' said Thorndyke. 'The death was properly certified, the deceased is buried, and you have not a single fact with which to support an application for further inquiry.'

'No,' Stalker agreed. 'But I am not satisfied. I don't believe the doctor really knew what she died from. I wish cremation were more usual.'

'So, I have no doubt, has many a poisoner,' Thorndyke remarked dryly.

But here is the first of the Holmes short stories, *A Scandal in Bohemia*, in which the King of Bohemia consults Sherlock Holmes:

'Your Majesty, as I understand, became entangled with this young person, wrote her some compromising letters, and is now desirous of getting those letters back.'

'Precisely so. But how—'

'Was there a secret marriage?'

'None.'

'No legal papers or certificates?'

'None.'

'Then I fail to follow your Majesty. If this young person should produce her letters for blackmailing or other purposes, how is she to prove their authenticity?'

'There is the writing.'

'Pooh, pooh! Forgery.'

'My private note-paper.'

'Stolen.'

'My own seal.'

'Imitated.'

'My photograph.'

'Bought.'

'We were both in the photograph.'

'Oh, dear! That is very bad! Your Majesty has indeed committed an indiscretion.'

'I was mad—insane.'

'You have compromised yourself seriously.'

'I was only Crown Prince then. I was young. I am but thirty now.'

'It must be recovered.'

'We have tried and failed.'

'Your Majesty must pay. It must be bought.'

'She will not sell.'

'Stolen, then.'

'Five attempts have been made. Twice burglars in my pay ransacked her house. Once we diverted her luggage when she travelled. Twice she has been waylaid. There has been no result.'

'No sign of it?'

'Absolutely none.'

Holmes laughed. 'It is quite a pretty little problem,' said he.

Freeman's first work of non-fiction, *Travels and Life in Ashanti and Jaman*, more than 500 pages long, was published in 1898 and was an account of an expedition to the North of what is now Ghana that he accompanied as assistant surgeon and naturalist ten years earlier. It is a surprising book, for although the purpose of the expedition was to incorporate Ashanti into a British protectorate, Freeman condemned British policy towards Ashanti as perfidious and counter-productive. He portrayed African life as far from being sunk in misery, even where ignorance prevailed, and called the British sack of the capital of the Ashanti kingdom, Kumasi, in 1873 barbaric.

Social Decay and Degeneration, published twenty three years later, and which he probably believed to be his masterpiece, is surprising for a different reason. Now he protests against the growing influence of the state, whose activities favour the unintelligent. His prescription, eugenics, is drastic—the intelligent are to be encouraged to breed and the unintelligent discouraged because:

'[T]he importance of the sub-man in the economy of society is not generally appreciated. The hindrance that he creates to the common welfare; his sinister influence in the present and the menace that he holds out to the future; are by the immense majority of persons completely unrecognised... the sub-man of our own race compares, on the whole, unfavourably with the average negro. But the negro race is admittedly inferior to any white race; so much so that at least one good observer has proposed to consider it as a sub-human species.'

The laudatory introduction to the book, incidentally, was written by the social reformer and writer of seven volumes of *Studies in the Psychology of Sex*, Henry Havelock Ellis (1859-1939), also a physician and one of the progenitors, if I may so put it, of the sexual revolution.

21

Goodness
The Conquest of Britain

It cannot be said that Hugh Williams, doctor of divinity and professor of church history at Bala College, the theological training establishment of the Welsh Independent Congregationalists, and author of *Christianity in Early Britain*, was a prose stylist. This book, his *magnum opus*, was published posthumously in 1912—he lived from 1843 to 1911—and is dry to the point of aridity, as if the author believed that to entertain the reader with either wit or anecdote were theological traps. He assumes not only the great importance of his subject, but that the reader has some pre-existing knowledge of it as well, including of Welsh (ancient Welsh at that), for there are entire passages in that language which he does not translate.

A reader of an article I wrote early in my career remarked that I did not write for the million. By contrast, Dr Williams did not write for the thousand. Still, his book was not completely without sustenance for the ignorant general reader such as I. My previous knowledge of its subject matter was exiguous, to say the least, and while I rather doubt that after having read 480 pages it will very much have increased, if it were tested, in a year's time, at least I will have a general outline of the history of early Christianity in Britain in my head.

In fact, I bought the book precisely because I was so ignorant of its subject. Like many others I have a tendency to read about those things on which I am already relatively well-informed, further reading on which will expand my knowledge only slightly, if at all, and will have the effect of strengthening my prejudices rather than of broadening my outlook. Nothing is more painful than having to change one's world outlook because of the acquisition of new knowledge.

Dr Williams did not permit himself many generalisations, nor was he given to aphoristic expression of ideas; but the following passage seems of startling relevance more than a century after it was published:

'Strange are the ways into which many of us fall, reflecting, as we do, the ideas and expressions of our own day, so familiar that they seem to have always existed, even in epochs and narratives of those epochs which did not know them.'

Now more than ever are we inclined to judge the past entirely in the light of our own moral values, as if we (in contrast to our forefathers) had finally alighted on the absolute moral truth. For us, the past is not another country where they do things differently, but our own nation. This would not be extraordinary were it not that we pride ourselves simultaneously on our cultural relativism and lack of prejudice in our own favour.

There is a conflict between moral absolutism and moral relativism which is not easy to resolve, because both have arguments in their support. Human nature is everywhere the same, which is why literature across the ages can speak to us. On the other hand, conduct which horrifies us did not horrify our ancestors, and seemed to them perfectly in keeping with morality. Their assumptions were not ours, and ours were not theirs, at least not in all respects. Whatever the metaphysics of moral judgment, our moral judgments are not true in the same way as it is true that, say, two and two make four.

Dr Williams encounters slight difficulties himself with historical judgment. He is described as completely even-handed in his treatment of early church history, but in *Christianity in Early Britain* he is clearly antagonistic (even if mildly) towards the apostolic claims of the Catholic church.[1] This is not surprisingly in view of his Welsh non-conformist background. He thought that the Catholic church increasingly usurped the authority of the independent native church of the Celtic west of Britain from about the time of St Augustine of Canterbury in 600 A.D., a usurpation from which his congregationalism followed by a kind of religious concatenation of its own. But whether his historical opinions followed from his religious opinions, or *vice versa*, I cannot say. His historical research could, of course, have confirmed to him that he happened to have been born into the correct faith.

For those of us without religious belief, the disputes of theologians seem a manifestation of our inclination to be quarrelsome. But so irreligious a man as Bertrand Russell was well-informed about the heresies and schisms of the early church which often had some important and still unresolved philosophical dispute underlying them. Despite his reservations about the Catholic church, Dr

Williams is at one with them in condemning Pelagius, the originator of the Pelagian heresy, who was born in Britain or Ireland sometime in the fourth century. And the Pelagian heresy—man is not born sinful—still resonates today.

When it comes to this dispute I sympathise with both, though I incline to the anti-Pelagian side. Pelagius seems to have been a proto-Rousseauian, because if man is not born sinful it has to be explained why he so often ends up as such—if his badness does not come from his inherent nature, where does it come from? What is the attraction to him of all that is morally forbidden? Rousseau says that man is born good but that society corrupts him. But how is it that society can corrupt creatures who are by nature good?

I don't take the story of the Garden of Eden literally, of course, but it seems to me that it is one of the most powerful metaphors ever imagined. I take it that all men and women subsequent to the expulsion are born with competing and irreconcilable desires and wishes, and that these desires and wishes inevitably push them sometimes to do what they ought not to do. Because of our nature, our perfect existence does not exist and is even inconceivable.[2] That is why depictions of hell are almost so much more passionately-imagined than those of heaven. We can each of us conceive of a thousand intolerable eternities, but our attempts to imagine eternal bliss are by contrast feeble, inclining to never-ending cruises on luxury liners, with eternal sunshine, calm seas, a choice of entertainment, no taxes and five excellent meals a day, etc.

I had patients who, as soon as they were able to, invariably made the worst choices. They were cruel early in their lives to animals, enjoying the infliction of suffering; they stole, lied and bullied as if no other conduct were possible for them. Evil exerted an attraction for them as a magnet for an iron filing; they treated the world and everyone in it as mere instruments for their use. They were neither happy nor even content, except fleetingly and always at the expense of others. But it never occurred to them in their discontent to try a different way to behave. Like Luther, they could do no other.[3]

What is less often noticed is that there are people at the other end of the moral spectrum. They are kindly, generous, even-tempered, charitable in their thoughts. They sometimes emerge from the most unpropitious circumstances. I remember a patient of mine, an alcoholic woman who carried her squalor around with her like the rings of Saturn. Her behaviour in drink was vile, and she was seldom not in drink. She lived in the kind of housing that is often called social, but which, thanks to persons such as she, should really be called antisocial. She had a son aged about seventeen or eighteen with whom she lived (there was no father) and with whom I talked after she had been admitted to hospital for self-inflicted injuries.

I had expected to meet an aggressive, sullen or resentful youth, but instead I met a young man of the sweetest disposition (not in any way cloying), who looked after his mother devotedly, cleaning up after her, attending to her needs or more likely to her whims, at the same time diligently and successfully pursuing his own education. He carried his goodness with him as his mother carried her squalor; and it seemed to me unlikely that anything in his environment or experience could have accounted for it. He was born good.

There is, it seems to me, a propensity to do good or evil which has a normal distribution in a population, but the balance can be shifted by circumstances in the direction either. Hugh Williams tells us in *Christianity in Early Britain* that, until its takeover by Rome after a long period of isolation, the British (i.e. Celtic) church was strong on monks and weak on bishops, suggesting that monasticism was a key.

Williams first came to prominence as the translator of *De Excidio et Conquestu Britanniae*, of the ruin of Britain, written by St Gildas, a monk, in the sixth century, first printed in the sixteenth, and finally translated in the nineteenth by Williams. St Gildas was born in Wales and has been called a tenth-rate Jeremiah[4] because of his strident denunciations, rather than contemplative nature, such as: 'Priests Britain has, but foolish ones; a great number of ministers, but shameless; pastors it has, so to say, but they are wolves ready for the slaughter of souls, certainly not providing what is of benefit for the people, but seeking the filling of their own belly; men have churches, but enter them for the sake of filthy lucre... in great numbers like men soaked in wine through drunkenness.'

I first came across monasticism when I was hitch-hiking through France as a teenager and some monks put me up in their monastery overnight. I had expected them to be solemn, but they were both kindly and jolly, and I had never met a group of men who seemed so content (nor have I met many since). Little did I suspect that I was witnessing the last gasp of a life on the verge of extinction. Most of those monks would not have been replaced. I thought then there would always be monks and monasteries because there had always been monks and monasteries.

Some forty years later I visited an ancient convent in Belgium, all but empty except for a few nuns waiting to die, none of them younger than their mid-eighties.[5] They reminded me of the last known Tasmanian tiger that died in a zoo in Hobart in 1936. When I wrote an article in which I said that monks and nuns in Africa—Spanish, Irish, German and Swiss—were the finest and most selfless people I had ever met, among the very few who seemed genuinely to love humanity, the response from readers was of a virulent hatred (particularly of nuns) that I had not at all expected.

I conceived by the end of the book a high regard for Hugh Williams. All erudition is hard-won, of course, but his was particularly hard-won, for he started life impoverished and spent several years as a mason, studying after hours of hard physical labour, and eventually producing a book in which he quoted in Welsh, English, French, German, Latin and Greek. He might not have been much fun to be with—a murderer who, having cut his best friend into pieces, once replied when asked to describe his character, 'I'm kind of laid-back and fun to be with'—but he was deeply serious in a way that I have never been. As I read his book, not always by any means enthralled, I heard a small voice of reproach at my own path through life.

1   Dr Williams is always reluctant to give the Bishops of Rome the title of Pope.

2   This is the whole point of Dr Johnson's great philosophical fable, *Rasselas*.

3   Luther's inability to do other than he did was, of course, because of a moral obligation, not because of a quasi-biological impulse.

4   A role I do not altogether despise as have often played it myself.

5   The way of life was obviously very healthy. The convent had a cemetery, and few of the nuns, whose tombs recorded only their religious names and their dates of birth and death, died aged less than ninety.

22

Truth
Criticism that Truly Stings

From Tenby to Carmarthen is only twenty-six miles. The countryside is pleasantly rolling, though one cannot say that the twentieth century has done much to improve it. But what would once have been a very full day's journey now takes thirty-six minutes.

One of the causes of my happy memories was that, unusually for a town so small, Carmarthen has two second-hand booksellers. In a way, it is only appropriate that the town should be unusual in this fashion, for it has a distinguished literary history. To take only one of them. It was in Carmarthen that the great Anglo-Welsh poet, R.S. Thomas, published his first collection of poems in 1947.[1] I first became interested in this angular curmudgeon when my wife was a locum in Wales.

From one of these shops, Carmarthen Rare Books, I bought such interesting volumes as eighteenth-century denunciations of the impostures of physicians and the uselessness of medication. I was at the time writing a weekly column in the *British Medical Journal* about the connections between medicine and literature. When first invited to write the column, my wife was worried that I would not be able to find enough material to last more than a few weeks or months. I discovered to my delight by much browsing, however, that the problem was more one of selection from the embarrassment of riches than of finding something to write about.

I love Carmarthen, though I dare say few people would find much to love about it. Even its best early-nineteenth-century buildings are rather run-down. One knows at once on entering it that this is an amphetamine- rather than a heroin-town for the so inclined. In Carmarthen you need stimulation rather than calming, and amphetamine will give you that illusion. There is a feeling that nothing can or will happen here, unless it be a sordid murder that acts like a flash of lightning on a completely darkened landscape.

Alas, Carmarthen Rare Books was closed on the day we arrived again in town. I suppose the number of passers-by in South-West Wales who are looking for eighteenth century exposures of the defects of medical science and its practitioners must be rather limited and declining.

Mrs Lloyd-Davies's shop, however, was open, if you rang first to let her know that you were coming. Hers is not exactly a shop, rather a terraced house filled with books, not all of them on shelves. I hope she will not mind if I say that she seems in some danger of being overwhelmed, if not actually evicted or displaced, by her books. She has the deep gravelly voice of one who indulges in habits that all doctors such as I are officially called upon to reprehend, but which in her case gives the impression of character and enjoyment of life. I was not surprised to learn that her son was a high-flier, fluent in Japanese and Chinese, living and working as far away from Carmarthen as possible, without actually leaving the surface of the planet.

With a cup of coffee precariously in hand, ready to put down somewhere and then not be able to find again, I scoured the familiar shelves between which I squeezed myself, my heart racing as I suppose hunters' hearts must race when they close in on a wounded but still ferocious beast. Of course, many of the books I had seen before (several times), for the trade in such books is a slow one— though I had bought a little collection from Mrs Lloyd-Davies on books offering cures to sufferers from consumption at a time when real cures did not yet exist.[2]

After two hours of happy browsing (one never knows a shelf of books as well as one thinks one does), I selected three books for purchase: the first, a first edition of Isaiah Berlin's famous lecture at the London School of Economics in 1953, *Historical Inevitability*, with a copy inside of Isaac Deutscher's famously damning review in the *Observer*. I had read a fair bit of Isaiah Berlin, including his *Four Essays on Liberty*, his essays on Vico, Herder, de Maistre, and Russian thinkers such as Belinsky and Chernyshevsky, as well as his biographical study of Marx and his translation of Turgenev's *First Love*. I had never read, at least as far as I recalled, *Historical Inevitability*, which, though it is hard to summarise, is not easy entirely to forget.

When I read Berlin I was an admirer of his style, his fluency, his range, and his obvious attachment to civilised values, but it is sometimes a mistake to return to an author whom one has uncritically admired at an earlier stage of one's life. Either *Historical Inevitability* was not one of Berlin's best works, or my admiration had been that of a rather easily impressionable person. The range and fluency are there all right, but one begins to wonder to what purpose.

The booklet, as printed, is seventy-eight densely-spaced pages of paragraphs as long as some people's essays, and cannot (surely?) be the mere transcript of the lecture as delivered. If it were, one might pity the poor listener. Even with Berlin's machine-gun delivery, it must have lasted several hours. His enunciation was famously clear, but it is hard enough to keep up with his cascading phrases on the printed page, let alone when heard for the first and last time, without possibility of return to what had been said.

Sometimes his lecture reads like the speech of a person in the early phase of manic-depression, for the words tumble over one another in what Deutscher in his review called 'this brilliant, irresistibly eloquent tirade... [a] tempestuous and rapid and roaring... hurricane fire'.

It is true that Berlin manages (just) to keep to the subject, that he does not indulge in what are called 'clang associations', the linking of ideas by means of the sound of words rather than of the progression of ideas, such as manics employ uncontrollably, but still one has the impression of a man whose speech is limping after his thoughts, never quite catching up with them. One cannot help but recall Michael Oakeshott's introduction of him to an audience at the London School of Economics as 'the Paganini of ideas', a perfect insult in so far as it could also be construed as a compliment. Berlin—amiable, clubbable, sociable—did not forget or forgive.

Berlin's attack on the notion of historical inevitability

seems to have been motivated more by an awareness of its terrible moral and practical consequences than by its untruth (though he does also believe it to be untrue). He was himself a refugee from the October Revolution led by a man, Lenin, who believed himself to be the instrument of history, justifying his own ferocity by the supposed transcendent denouement of that history that would lead—via the elimination of whole classes of merchants, industrialists, philosophers, priests—to the sunny uplands of perpetual peace and plenty. Berlin had relatives left behind in Russia, who suffered or died under both the Communists and the Nazis, that is to say under two ideologies that claimed to be fulfilling the dictates of history. He had good personal reason to mistrust the belief in historical inevitability.

My brush with historical inevitability occurred in Africa. As a young doctor I went to work in what was still called Rhodesia (now Zimbabwe). Rhodesia was then a state run entirely by a small racial and colonial minority led by Ian Smith. Irrespective of the rights and wrongs of the situation, and whether a change of regime would be to the benefit or detriment of the population as a whole, it was clear to me that the present situation was untenable and that the regime could not last. The winds of change had blown and the tiny minority could not long hold out against the rest of the world.

Of course, Ian Smith did not think so. When I met him at a garden party (he was a modest and well-mannered man), he asked me how long I was staying in the country and when I told him it was for only a few months, he said,

'Stay a lifetime, man.' He plainly thought that Rhodesia was a land of opportunity for such as I. Not long afterwards, I witnessed the arrival of the first white soldier who was wounded and evacuated to a hospital in Bulawayo, an event which was then regarded as a curiosity but which I, young as I was, thought was a harbinger of inevitable change.

It is one thing, however, to predict an outcome in a particular situation and another entirely to say that the whole of human history has an inevitable end to which it is moving either fast or slow, with sudden periods of acceleration or revolutions. Even worse is it for individuals to perform acts which would normally be condemned for their violence or cruelty on the grounds that they are acting according to history's dictates and are therefore not truly responsible for what they do. Lenin's ethics, that everything was permissible or obligatory that furthered the revolution and the cause of the working class, and everything immoral (and futile) that delayed its eventual and inevitable triumph, were responsible for tens of millions of deaths, and perfectly compatible with any number of deaths and any amount of suffering.[3] It was this deeply repellent philosophy that Berlin, with his magniloquent indirection, was concerned to refute.

In essence, this philosophy, in somewhat devious form, was Isaac Deutscher's. Like Berlin, Deutscher was a refugee, though he arrived in Britain from Poland too late in life to lose his accent. That made his accomplishment of an elegant prose style in English (his third or fourth language) all the most admirable.[4] Though he believed that Stalin had distorted Lenin's legacy, he nevertheless was an apologist for the Soviet Union, at least by comparison with the West. He was slippery and evasive when it came to the horrors of Communism.

Berlin considered him to be thoroughly dishonest as a scholar and, worse still, a conscious apologist for ultimate evil. It was Berlin who prevented Deutscher from ever being employed by a British university, saying that he was the one man whose presence he would find intolerable in a department in which he, Berlin, worked.[5] In effect, he blackballed Deutscher from British academic life at a time when it resembled a club. Berlin did not object to the employment of Marxists as such, it was Deutscher's employment specifically to which he objected. The source of that animus was Deutscher's *Observer* review of Berlin's *Historical Inevitability*, included with my copy. It was the last paragraph of the review that wounded his vanity: 'But Mr Berlin does not analyse. He does not even argue his case. He proclaims and declaims it. Like some other great rhetoricians, he is not over-scrupulous or even over-precise in his statements.'

No criticism is a fraction as hurtful as the justified.

---

1   *The Stones of the Field*, 1946, Druid Press. The press was situated above a shop and run by the poet and editor, Keidrych Rhys.

2   My favourite was *The Treatment of Tuberculosis with Umckaloabo (Stevens's Cure)* by Dr Adrien Sechehaye. Stevens was Charles Henry Stevens, born in 1880 in Birmingham, who went out aged seventeen to South Africa to be cured of his pulmonary tuberculosis. There he claimed to have been cured by an African healer with root of the African geranium, *pelargonium siloides*. Stevens decided to market *umckaloabo* (a name that he may well have concocted himself, and which to my ears at least conjures up a pretty foul-tasting concoction) and had considerable success. In 1909, the British Medical Association included *umckaloabo* in its famous book

exposing quack cures, *Secret Remedies* (practically all 'legitimate' medicines at the time would now be considered quack remedies). Stevens sued for libel in 1912. The first jury could not agree, the second found for the BMA and awarded £2000 against Stevens who was refused a third trial. I doubt that he was straightforwardly a fraud; and his remedy continued to be sold. Indeed, it still has its advocates among enthusiasts of alternative medicine, and there is a little evidence that it might be of slight use in upper respiratory tract infections. Curiously enough, the file on *umckaloabo* held in the Wellcome Institute Library (which has material dating up to 1936) is said to be very sensitive and is closed until 1 January, 2089. What can be so sensitive? Clearly, I was born before my time.

3   He shared this remarkable accomplishment with a much greater writer of Polish origin, Joseph Conrad, and with one of Hungarian provenance, Arthur Koestler. Both of these took a diametrically opposite view of the Revolution to Deutscher's, Koestler turning against it after a period of youthful approval.

4   To the end of his days my father, who died at an age twenty years older than could read and pronounce Hebrew as fluently as he could read English, though he understood hardly a word of it, and went decades without practice. The same was true of my paternal uncles. Arthur Koestler, the product of a much more secularised family than that in which Deutscher claimed to have grown up, was the inventor of crosswords in Hebrew.

5   By strange coincidence, I was appointed Max Hartwell Scholar-in-Residence for a month at the Centre for Independent Studies in Sydney shortly after I read *Historical Inevitability*. Hartwell was an Australian economic historian who spent most of his academic life in Oxford. He had a famous dispute—famous, that is, in the small circles of economic historians—with the Marxist historian Eric Hobsbawm. Hartwell maintained that the Industrial Revolution had raised the level of consumption of the poor in Britain, while Hobsbawm maintained the opposite. Hartwell is generally believed to have prevailed, though having been right does not guarantee subsequent fame. Hartwell had moved to Oxford largely as a protest against the refusal of an Australian university to appoint a Marxist historian for purely ideological reasons.

23

Consciousness
'I say, Jeeves'

I don't suppose Isaac Deutscher would have derived very much pleasure from the work of P.G. Wodehouse. Bertie Wooster, the featherbrained upper-class nincompoop, has a large private income ultimately derived (and perhaps not even ultimately, but almost immediately) from the blood, sweat and tears of the workers, that is to say from the surplus value extracted (again, ultimately or not) by force from their labour.

This, of course, has always been the way of ruling classes. But what is particularly true about Wooster is that he does not even fulfil the cultural function of past ruling classes. He does not patronise the arts either with money or by knowledge and connoisseurship. He is a philistine whose highest aesthetic aspiration is a pair of spats in Old-Etonian colours, or a pair of startlingly purple socks. His underling Jeeves has to rein in his excursions into patronage of shirtmakers and tailors, for Wooster has lost even the instinct for beauty that might once have marked members of his class, thereby justifying (to a very minor extent) their existence. Wooster is the archetype of the decline into utter decadence of that class. As feeble as a litter of new-born kittens, it has not the mental power even to appreciate the danger it is in.

As for Jeeves, the valet (or, in Deutscher's terms, the lackey) who is forever saving Wooster from the consequences of his own idiocies, he is the classical class traitor who exchanges his birth-right, for the Woosterian mess of pottage or (to change the metaphor slightly) the crumbs from the rich man's table. It is no accident that Jeeves is so much more intelligent than Wooster, for he has on his side, whether he likes, or knows it, or not, the wisdom derived ultimately from one's class position in society.[1] In Marxist terms, Jeeves is automatically, *ex officio* as it were, endowed with more intelligence than Wooster.

The problem is that Jeeves fails to apply it properly. It remains to be explained why, with a world to win, he hitches his wagon to so obviously decrepit and futureless a locomotive as Wooster. After all, the episodes in *The Inimitable Jeeves* (a first edition, published in 1923, of which I found on Mrs Lloyd-Davies's shelves) took place after the end of the Great War and after the Bolshevik Revolution. The old order could not stand and light the path to the future. Yet Jeeves, who was not stupid, took no notice of the writing on the wall, and continued to behave as if the choice of tie and cufflinks were most important choices a man could ever face.

Jeeves could have believed in the revolution that would make redundant the *métier* of valet and would give him perhaps the post of Commissar of Fashion, but he might well have estimated that it would not occur in his lifetime and that therefore he was better off as he was—*Après Jeeves le déluge*. Another interpretation is that Jeeves was suffering from what Marxists call 'false consciousness'. This is a bit like the Stockholm syndrome, in which, through an attempt to reconcile himself with his own powerlessness, the person kidnapped comes to see the world through his kidnappers' eyes. Jeeves pretends to like Wooster and to be genuinely concerned for his welfare, notwithstanding the evident worthlessness of Wooster's existence. Here Marxism touches Freudianism in that a man's true motives are opaque to himself.

What of their real creator, Pelham George Wodehouse? Wodehouse was born into the lower reaches of the upper-middle class (like George Orwell). He feared being *déclassé* and, like Jeeves, identified entirely with the world of Wooster. Fending off awareness of the decline of his favoured class, he created a seemingly timeless and changeless existence in which conflict, in so far as it existed, was a matter for humour rather than for serious analysis, and was the consequence not of opposing material interests and forces but of personal affairs, such as love.

Unlike the imagined Marxist attack on Jeeves above, and his defence, Wodehouse was in real life decried as a traitor during and after the war for having made the Berlin broadcasts, directed to America, after his capture by the Germans at his house in Le Touquet, France. In real life he reached for a similar rebuttal, that he was ignorant of the ideological politics of the century.

Although Wodehouse's oeuvre is immense, he was not a mere hack who churned out pages by a process of quasi-industrial production. 'I took care', he said, referring to his own writing; and he was a stylist, as the following short passage from *The Inimitable Jeeves* demonstrates. The soufflé-brained Wooster addresses Jeeves:

> 'I say, Jeeves, a man I met at the club last night told me to put my shirt on Privateer for the two o'clock race this afternoon. How about it?'
>
> 'I should not advocate it, sir. The stable is not sanguine.'
>
> That was enough for me. Jeeves knows. How, I couldn't say, but he knows.

Regardless of Wodehouse's claim to be a political novice, Deutscher would have sniffed out immediately in *The Inimitable Jeeves* that Wodehouse was an ideological enemy.[2] The story made fun of Communism in 1923, only six years after the Bolshevik Revolution and when world revolution was still a possibility.

In *The Inimitable Jeeves*, another young parasite called Bingo Little is Wooster's best friend. His main characteristic, other than his almost militant social parasitism, is his propensity to fall in and out of love with a succession of young women, often of the lower orders. He falls in love, on the top of a bus, with one Charlotte Corday Rowbotham, so named by her Communist father in honour of the assassin of Marat. Bingo Little's only hope of pursuing the affair, and to meet with the approval of Rowbotham *père*, is to pose himself as a Communist. He adopts a false beard and mounts a soap box at Speakers' Corner to issue bloodcurdling threats against the bourgeoisie.

Wooster's description of Speaker's Corner took me back fifty years when, on Sunday afternoons, I used to frequent it as a listener. The Corner was, 'where weird birds of every description collect on Sunday afternoons and stand on soap boxes and make speeches... an atheist was letting himself go with a good deal of vim, while in front of him there stood a little group of serious thinkers with a banner labelled "Heralds of the Red Dawn".' In my days at the Corner there was a 'weird bird' who exposed himself in all weathers because every inch of his body was covered in tattoos, to the appalled and delighted derision of the onlookers.

Bingo Little, in his disguise as a Communist revolution-ary, makes a speech in which he points at Wooster, who is in the company of Little's own father, Lord Bittlesham:

'Yes, look at them! Drink them in!' he was yelling, his voice rising above the perpetual motion fellow's and beating the missionary service all to nothing. 'There you see two typical members of this class which has downtrodden the poor for centuries. Idlers! Non-producers! Look at the tall one with the face like a motor-mascot. Has he ever done an honest day's work in his life? No! A prowler, a trifler, and a blood-sucker! And I bet he still owes his tailor for those trousers!'

Unfortunately for Bingo Little, Comrade Butt of the Red Dawn is his rival for the affections of Charlotte. In order to help him in his pursuit, Wooster asks the members of the Red Dawn, including Charlotte's father and

Comrade Butt, to tea in his flat off Piccadilly.

'Mr Wooster?' said old Rowbotham. 'May I say Comrade Wooster?'

'I beg your pardon?'

'Are you of the movement?'

'Well—er—'

'Do you yearn for the Revolution?'

'Well, I don't know that I exactly yearn. I mean as far as I can make out, the whole nub of the scheme seems to be to massacre coves like me; and I don't mind owning I'm not frightfully keen on the idea.'

'But I'm talking him round,' said Bingo. 'I'm wrestling with him. A few more treatments might do the trick.'

Old Rowbotham looked at me a bit doubtfully. 'Comrade Little has great eloquence,' he admitted....

[Meanwhile Butt] was scowling in a morose sort of manner at young Bingo and the girl, who were giggling together by the window. 'I wonder the food didn't turn to ashes in our mouths! Eggs! Muffins! Sardines! All wrung from the bleeding lips of the starving poor!'

The Inimitable Jeeves demonstrates that Wodehouse was exquisitely sensitive to the political currents of his time and under a Leninist-Stalinist regime—on such regimes' past performance—his novel would have been more than sufficient to fit the crime of 'treason'. His broadcasts were implicit endorsements of the Nazi regime, as if it was unexceptional.[3] Like William Joyce (Lord Haw-Haw), he would have been hanged and one assumes Deutscher would have seen no problem with this.[4]

Secretly I have to admit I am sufficiently puritanical to believe that everyone should contribute what he can to the welfare of society and that Wooster is a murky character. I have no objection either to great wealth or inherited great wealth, but they do bring their obligations, and employing Jeeves is not quite enough.

I suppose I should not have had this po-faced reaction myself had I found *The Inimitable Jeeves* a great deal funnier. At best it made me smile, and then only a few times.

[1]   'The mode of production of material life conditions the general process of social, political and intellectual life. It is not the consciousness of men that determines their existence, but their social existence that determines their consciousness.' Karl Marx, preface to *A Contribution to the Critique of Political Economy*.

[2]   Even the habit or custom of naming children after revolutionary heroes, as once children were named after saints, is recognised. Carlos the Jackal, Illich Ramírez Sánchez, was given his first name in commemoration of the butchering intellectual who led the October Revolution.

[3]   At the time Wodehouse made his famous, or infamous, broadcasts, Nazi Germany and the Soviet Union were allies rather than enemies. But Deutscher, with his subtle dialectical mind, would have been able easily to explain this away. He would have said that in making a pact with Hitler, in occupying the Baltic States and half of Poland, in perpetrating the Katyn Massacre of the Polish officer class and intelligentsia,, who were the enemies of the Polish working class and incipient collaborators with Nazism, he was merely buying time to prepare the Soviet Union's defences against the real enemy, whom he knew all along to be Nazi Germany. As Karl Popper pointed out a long time ago, dialectics of the Hegelian-Marxist kind means that any proposition can be reconciled with any other. When it comes to rationalisation, however, we are all master dialecticians.

[4]   William Joyce was not a traitor to Britain because he was not a British subject. It was, in effect, his English accent that hanged him.

24

Excess
Holy Fools

I doubt whether much can be done to restore the reputation of William Le Queux, described as 'novelist and self-publicist.' Though, as we are all self-publicists now through social media, perhaps a new, posthumous career lies ahead. A person is expected to 'big himself up', to use the expressive phrase I heard from some of my patients.

If all modesty is false, one can't help but admire a man who was born in 1864 as the son of a French immigrant draper's assistant and who rose to wealth and celebrity by writing more than two hundred books, and who claimed among his readers not only royalty and the upper echelons of the political class (including three Prime Ministers, the notoriously high-minded and severely intellectual A.J. Balfour, Herbert Henry Asquith, and Lloyd George), but also the young Graham Greene. In his autobiography, *Things I Know about Kings, Celebrities and Crooks*, published four years before his death in 1927, he does not so much name-drop as -pelt, and yet he is under no illusion as to the value of his own work.

He says he has always refused to call himself a man of letters, and: 'I am, alas! only too well aware of my own failings, of my hopeless grammar.' His excuse for his bad grammar is that he only 'at times tried to entertain… with healthy, if exciting, fiction'—bearing titles such as *A Secret Sin*, *The Indiscretions of a Lady's Maid*, *Sins of the City* and *Wiles of the Wicked*.

Le Queux's mind was essentially trashy and happily and cheerfully so. The dust-jacket of his *Rasputin the Rascal Monk* (published during the October Revolution in 1917), which I also bought at Mrs Lloyd's, reflects this. Printed on poor-quality paper and badly sewn, it was published while the Great War was still in progress.

My copy, one of the 110,000 to be printed, still has its dust jacket, in good condition despite its fragility, on which appears a picture on a white ground of a sinister Rasputin, half-Svengali, half-Fagin (with the eyes of Hitler), staring hypnotically out at the reader with the outline of a *pickelhuber* (the German spiked helmet), in gold and black, behind him. To his right a clutch of naked female arms, obviously those of the society women who were in thrall to him, reach out towards him. To his left, the black imperial eagle of Germany drops gold coins on to a little pyramid of such coins. On the back of the dust-jacket is an advertisement for Fry's Pure Breakfast Cocoa, 'loved by the bairnies', with a picture of a little curly-headed girl, 'the lucky one!', holding a mug of chocolate while two disappointed children look on.

Le Queux claims to have met Rasputin before the days of his world-notoriety, in a village called Alexandrovsk on the Arctic Circle. He had 'remarkable steel-grey eyes' and his appearance was 'distinctly uncleanly.' Before he founded what amounted to a gnostic sect, Rasputin was 'a mere illiterate *mujik* [peasant]. Disgusting in his habits and bestial in his manners, [he] grew lazy and dissolute, taking to theft and highway-robbery... for which he was imprisoned twice... he suddenly conceived the brilliant idea of posing as a "holy man". The idea came to him because, while in Pokrovsky, he had as a boon companion and fellow-drunkard a certain market-gardener who had joined the Pravoslavny Church and is today by his influence actually a bishop!'

The most interesting idea in the book is that Rasputin exerted his influence over the illness of the Tsarevich (haemophilia) by pharmacological means. According to Le Queux, Rasputin was well-versed in the arcane medical lore of Tibet and arranged for the Tsarevich to be given a secret medicament by a close friend of the Empress's Anna Vyrubova, who was also his acolyte, in order to provoke the Tsarevich's bleeding. Rasputin would then arrive providentially, and the bleeding would stop as the natural consequence of the Tsarevich being given the medicament no more. For this theory there is no evidence whatsoever, other than that it was first put forward by Iliodor, an Orthodox priest who had once been a friend of Rasputin's. The priest turned against him, even involving himself in an unsuccessful plot to assassinate his former friend, and calling him 'the Holy Devil', the title of the book that he wrote about him.

I had a certain sympathy for the theory because I once proposed a similar theory as a solution to the puzzle of the illness of the King of France in *All's Well that Ends Well*. Helena, the daughter of a famous but recently deceased physician of Narbonne, has inherited his recipe for an ointment that is a panacea, while the French king suffers from a fistula that his physicians cannot cure and from which he is thought (not least by himself) to be dying. Helena goes to him and offers to cure him; if she fails she will be executed, but if she succeeds she will have the choice of any husband she wishes within the power of the king to grant. Many a dying patient has tried a crankish remedy on precisely this argument, and who can entirely blame them? But in fact the king, though ill and likely to die eventually is at no immediate risk of death, and therefore Helena must be confident that, at the very least, her remedy (an ointment) will do no harm.

As it happens, William Le Queux had both a self-proclaimed interest in toxicology and a keen appreciation of the value of placebos. His book, *The Death Doctor*, published in 1912, called by some 'his most repulsive fiction,' and therefore the one that I most assiduously sought out, is full of both poisons and placebos. The picture that Le Queux paints of my profession in the book is hardly a flattering one. Doctors are either gullible fools or murderous psychopaths. The book purports to be the posthumous memoirs of Archibald More d'Escombe, M.D., as edited and published by Laurence Lanner-Brown, M.D. One cannot help wondering whether Le Queux had something against the British medical profession.

Dr Lanner-Brown is the unsuspecting dupe of his professional colleague, whom he does not in the least suspect, until he inherits his manuscript of poisoning his patients by various arcane methods, from anthrax in soap, diphtheria in cigars, pneumococcus by injection and by spray in a respirator, rabies in ointment, glanders by a pin inserted in a pair of gloves, tetanus in soap, typhoid on sweets, anthrax by needle, and scarlet fever by infected fomites of skin, to strychnine and cocaine by injection, apomorphine and calabar-bean extract to induce uncontrollable and fatal vomiting in an alcoholic, and hyoscamine and nicotine poisoning (to kill his own wife).

Perhaps the most elaborate scheme is an injection of hyoscyamine that agitates a patient so severely that he strangles the very person whom Dr d'Escombe wants out of the way and then suffers amnesia. Le Queux's description of the pharmacological effects of this drug is accurate, but no one could possibly use hyoscyamine to procure a murder in this way, for though the agitation and confusion consequent upon the administration of the drug are predictable, the actions resulting from the confusion and agitation are not.

When Dr d'Escombe is not actually poisoning his patients, either at the behest of their relatives who pay him handsomely for his pains, or for his own direct benefit, he treats them always with placebos. When one contemplates the pharmacopoeia of the time, this approach seems a realistic choice for an intentional poisoner.

Le Queux seems to have gone through a textbook of both bacteriology and toxicology. He was familiar with Witthaus's *Manual of Toxicology*, for he mentions it in his autobiographical account of having met Dr Crippen, who called himself Dr Adams under an assumed name, before he, Crippen, became notorious for having poisoned his wife. According to the story, this 'Dr Adams' wrote to Le

Queux out of the blue, asking to meet him because he was interested in his work and had 'a new and exciting plot' to suggest to him.

'Poisoners,' confided Dr Adams to Le Queux, 'are always bunglers. The fools use arsenic, antimony, alkaloidal and glucosidal poisons under the illusion that they won't be found out.' Le Queux writes, 'I listened as he unfolded to me a most diabolical and ingenious plot, at which I sat aghast at the man's mentality. He had weighed every detail and taken every precaution so that there was no flaw.'

So aghast was Le Queux that he met Dr Adams several more times after the first. '[H]e unfolded to me many plots from his fertile brain, one of which, indeed, I did use later,' though he assures us 'in his presence I always felt a strong antipathy towards him.' Before long, 'he had explained so many means by which deadly poisons and bacteria of fatal diseases could be disseminated that at last, whenever I received a letter from him, I opened it with scissors, held it from me as I read it, and dropped it straight into the fire.' Only later, when his picture was published in all the newspapers, did Le Queux realise that Dr Adams was really Crippen.

Was any of this true? Certainly *The Death Doctor*, in which 'so many means by which deadly poisons and bacteria of fatal diseases' were disseminated, was published in the year following Dr Crippen's execution, but Le Queux, whose imagination was always inclined to the lurid, would hardly have needed Crippen to suggest outlandish plots to him. Le Queux was, if not entirely a fantasist, at least a man who always made the best of a small kernel of truth. He called himself a diplomat, which in a technical sense he was. For a time (until his bankruptcy occasioned by divorce), he was honorary consul of the Republic of San Marino in Birmingham and had a dazzling diplomatic uniform to show for it. But, what's San Marino to Birmingham, or Birmingham to San Marino?

There is no doubt, however, that he had an adventurous life; that he did hobnob with the minor royalty of Europe (for example the King of Montenegro) and that he travelled to remote places. It has even been suggested that he was instrumental in the foundation of MI5 and MI6.

In so far as he is remembered at all, it is for his book published in 1910 warning against the forthcoming war between Britain and Germany, for which the former was completely unprepared. Of course, if you make enough dire predictions, one or other of them is bound to come true. Of course, it also goes the other way. Early in *Things I Know*, published in the year following Mussolini's March on Rome, Le Queux describes an audience with King Victor Emmanuel of Italy who 'had welcomed with open hand Signor Mussolini, and the splendid Italian Fascisti, who are known as the "Black Shirts".'

One cannot blame Le Queux for trying to find a rational explanation of the sway that Rasputin undoubtedly had over the haemophilia of the Tsarevich, even if his theory of timely poisoning by Anna Vyrubova does not hold water. Coincidence might explain it if there were only one or two episodes of Rasputin's influence bringing about an end to the Tsarevich's haemorrhagic crises, but there are at least eight such episodes, one of them so serious that last rites had been read over the bed in which he had been prostrated for days. It has been suggested that Rasputin's influence calmed the Tsarina's overwrought nerves, and that his calming influence extended itself through her to the Tsarevich, whose blood pressure would have decreased, leading to less profuse bleeding. This seems far-fetched. Nevertheless, there must be some psychosomatic explanation of Rasputin's influence on the Tsarevich's haemorrhages, and this in itself would be a proper subject for research were it not that so adequate a physiological treatment for haemophilia now exists.

Le Queux makes no attempt to explain Rasputin's influence over the Tsar and his wife, as well as over many society ladies, except by reference to their atavistic superstition and ignorance. Popular writers such as he must clear their pages, and no doubt their minds as well, of subtlety, complication and any of the inherent ambiguities of life.

By Rasputin's time, however, Russia had had a centuries-old tradition of ignorant peasants, dirty and unkempt, often mentally handicapped or ill, as was Rasputin, taking to the road, behaving in a disagreeable and even reprehensible manner, and being taken as holy fools for Christ's sake. Indeed, the worse and more irresponsibly they behaved, the holier they were deemed to be. 'A holy fool was not an ordinary sinner but a holy sinner, pure and impure at the same time,' wrote Ewa M. Thompson in her excellent *Understanding Russia: The Holy Fool in Russian Culture*. '[Holy sinners] purposefully dressed in a ridiculous way, led the lives of vagrants and performed scandalous deeds. They did so to perfect themselves spiritually.'

Holy fools were both powerless and powerful. They did not possess much but were believed to have oracular or occult powers. Only bad people treated them badly, that is to say with disdain, and such people risked retribution for doing so. Although holy fools were beggars and in that sense subordinate, they were not only respected but also feared by all strata of society because they 'were capable of scandalous and malicious actions against those who displeased or contradicted them… ruined reputations could result from an accusation levelled at someone by a holy fool.'

Of course, the phenomenon is not purely Russian. In John B. Keane's play about Irish rural and small town life in the 1950s, *Sithe*, two tinkers appear, dressed in eccentric costume, making oracular pronouncements and causing considerable fear in the other characters. My Irish friends tell me that the scene is extremely accurate (Keane, besides being a playwright, kept a pub in Listowel). And I remember gypsies coming to the door in London in the same decade, offering some slight service or other along with their blessing should it be accepted and paid for. The unspoken corollary of their offer was a curse if it was not accepted and paid for. Strangely enough, there lingered a slight fear that their curse might actually be of some effect, even though, normally speaking, we scorned the very idea or possibility of occult powers. And to this day, I have a faint residue of feeling that, if I do not give money to a beggar or accept to buy the merchandise or the services of those poor people whom come to my door, I will suffer some retribution from their curses.

25

Roles
Dylan Thomas

Our last stop from (and on our return to) Bridgnorth was in Laugharne, on the estuary of the River Tawe. This little town is now indissolubly linked with, and perhaps economically dependent upon, the memory of Dylan Thomas—itself as strong as ever.

Outwardly, little has changed except for some average modern houses overlooking the estuary. But in the intervening years between his death and now much has changed culturally.

For example, the Boathouse, the enchanting place bought for Dylan Thomas by Margaret Taylor,[1] where he and his wife and children lived from 1949 until his death in 1953, has long been a kind of shrine dedicated to him. Though some things, like health and safety, trump that veneration. The first time I visited the Boathouse, I was startled by the notice on its lavatory door: 'IT IS ILLEGAL TO SMOKE ON THESE PREMISES'.

Dylan Thomas was, of course, a heavy smoker. I wonder when it will become illegal to publish a photograph of him with a cigarette between his lips or fingers? In France they managed pictoriographically to remove Albert Camus's cigarette.[2] Nor was he much of one for health and safety. Three notices on the stone path in plot adjacent to the house warned visitors, 'UNEVEN STEPS', while from the house boomed a recording of Thomas reading 'And Death Shall Have no Dominion'. Health and safety is non-conformist puritanism (with which Thomas was all-too familiar) with the religion removed. One delights to think what Thomas, who loved the rich absurdity of human beings, would have made of it all.

No one who has ever been to the Boathouse and looked out on the estuary from the veranda will ever forget the first stanza of 'Poem in October', or fail to recognise its precision and just and profound marking out of what makes this landscape so moving:

> And the mussel pooled and the heron
> Priested shore
> The morning beckon
> With water praying and call of seagull and rook
> And the knock of sailing boats on the net webbed wall.

Dylan Thomas is a figure who continues to intrigue me as the greatest regret of my life is that I was born too late to be a bohemian. He was one of the last generations before the revolution that made bohemianism so universal that it was no longer possible—counter-culture and out-landishness having become conformity. By the time I was old enough to be one, respectability had almost died out, and bohemianism is parasitic on respectability for its attraction. When everyone is a bohemian, no one is.

It never occurred to Thomas to get a regular job or nod to the restrictive conventions of the society into which he

was born. He considered employment only as a temporary
and regrettable expedient to get him out of a financial fix.
Drinking, sponging off others, indifference to social
niceties, womanising, physical squalor, petty theft (of
shirts, for example), and even not-so-petty theft, were his
mode of life. The notion of returning borrowed money
was so alien to him that it never even crossed his mind to
do so. He had no concept of *meum et tuum*. He bilked
tradesmen if he could, treated other people's homes
without respect, leaving them in a mess and unapologeti-
cally breaking their valuable furniture in quarrels with his
fiery wife, Caitlin.

The Oxford historian A.J.P. Taylor—no stickler for
convention himself—detested Thomas for his laziness,
dishonesty, drunkenness, and parasitism. It was his wife,
who, in love with Thomas, had given him the money to live
in the Boathouse. Yet Thomas was far from grateful for his
patron's largesse (she paid all his bills, too). In private he
was disparaging about, even contemptuous of her, and
regarded her cold-bloodedly as a cash cow.

When I was the right age to become a bohemian,
property prices had risen so much that it was no longer
possible to live in what one might call higher squalor in the
centre of a great city, renting a single uncomfortable room
for next to nothing. No one wants a feckless poet or
painter as a tenant, not even of a cupboard-size room.

Though I would like to have been a bohemian, but was
prevented by a natural timidity that reduced my unconven-
tionality to private gestures and never risked social obloquy,
I had a second cousin who lived such a life in Paris, residing

in the Hotel Louisiane on the rue de Seine, the haunt of the Beat Poets and the like, who was briefly the consort of Richard Wright, the author of *Native Son*.[3]

My father detested her and more or less forbade her the house, not because, in her green polo-necked sweater and red lipstick, she was a bad moral influence (she was very beautiful), but because he thought she was an artistic phony, as she thought him an intellectual one. It is probably easier to have two Napoleons in the same asylum than two people who consider each other phonies.[4] So I saw little of my cousin in my childhood—not that she was very keen on children anyway.

But whenever I think of bohemians, a picture of her comes irresistibly into my mind. She wrote a little poetry, some of which was published in tiny English-language magazines in Paris. I remember only one line from any of her poems, 'As mine as you are not'. Much later, she told me that she had thought that Richard Wright had been killed by the CIA. He had been treated for amoebic dysentery contracted in Africa in the American Hospital in Paris and died shortly thereafter. She was not best pleased when I suggested that it might have been the emetine hydrochloride, the drug of choice in those days for amoebic dysentery, and very cardiotoxic, that might have killed him.

If someone now dressed as my second cousin had done sixty years ago before she had the good sense to marry a very successful businessman, she would be considered unduly formal. Nowadays, it is sometimes difficult to distinguish by the mode of dress the chief executive of a giant corporation from a student and it is easier to express social rebellion by wearing a collar and tie than by turning up at a cocktail party in a turtleneck sweater, once regarded as the height of eccentricity. My cousin, instead, became a patroness to superannuated bohemians.

I would have wanted not only to be a bohemian, but a bohemian with talent. I would not have been satisfied with merely playing a part. To what extent did Dylan Thomas play a part?[5]

Thomas grew up in a respectable area of Swansea known as Uplands, in an Edwardian-style house on a street called Cwmdonkin Drive. The Thomas family had a maid and his father was head of English teaching at Swansea Grammar School at a time of high academic standards. Thomas Sr was a dissatisfied man, bitter that his talents had gone unrecognised—he once applied for the chair of English at Aberystwyth University College but was turned down in favour of someone he thought his inferior. Like V.S. Naipaul's father, Thomas Sr had unfulfilled literary aspirations, and vicarious social and academic ambitions for his son. He was a native Welsh speaker, for example, but did not want his son to learn the language, thinking this a worthless and even deleterious accomplishment that would mark Dylan as belonging to a culturally backward race. Indeed, he paid for the young Dylan to have elocution lessons, to expunge Welshness from his pronunciation.

The young Dylan set about frustrating his father's ambitions for him. He attended the grammar school in which his father taught; but he was an undisciplined scholar, and his formal education ceased when he was sixteen. Thomas was a quart that could not be fit into a pint pot.

There is no doubt that he liked an audience and early in his life wore clothes that he thought poets (as compared with, say, bank clerks) wore. But it is obvious from Thomas's biography that he could never have pursued any ordinary career. If anyone were by some genetic quirk ever be a born bohemian, it was he.

He early conceived the vocation of poet, as others conceive a religious vocation. At thirteen, he published a poem in a South-Wales newspaper, though (as was later discovered) it was pure plagiarism. For a long time, Dylan Thomas was as famous for his life as for his works; his roistering, drunken, undisciplined existence exerted an attraction for people chained by circumstance or cowardice to the humdrum world of getting and spending. That Thomas for much of his short life received an income from his writing that would have been adequate for comfort, if only he spent it wisely; that he never took buses but only taxis, even when broke and even for long distances and at immense expense; that he sent his son to be privately educated—none of this was widely known, for poverty as a consequence of his principled determination to live as a poet was more appropriate to the legend he created and lived.

Thomas may have played the part of the doomed poet, but he was a genius. Few are the twentieth-century English poets who wrote lines that not only were memorable but that also make the soul vibrate. Thomas was one of them.

I bought two books in the Boathouse bookstall, one of them Caitlin Thomas's fourth memoir of her marriage to

Dylan, *Double Drink Story*. The other was *Dylan Thomas and the Bohemians: The Photographs of Nora Summers* by Gabriel Summers and Leonie Summers with Jeff Towns.

I am never quite sure what 'with' means in a list of authors, but I knew Jeff Towns slightly. When we had stayed in South-West Wales, in Carmarthen or Llanelli, I used to visit his second-hand and antiquarian bookshop in Swansea. I quickly learned that he was one of the world's great experts on the life and work of Dylan Thomas, and of course on its bibliography, though he was knowledge-able about much else beside. English from the East End of London, he started to deal in books straight out of university and had specialised in Dylan Thomas for more than forty years, accumulating a large collection of his own, destined for America because, apart from having more money, the Americans have more interest in and respect for literary history. He had a tenacity of character that I do not have and wished that I did.

I shall always be grateful to him for having introduced me to a Welsh writer of whom I had not even heard, though he was reasonably well known up until his death in the 1970s—Rhys Davies, now undeservedly forgotten. My own greatest literary achievement is having encouraged a German publisher, who read my essay on Davies, to have some of his work translated into German.

The two books, *Double Drink Story* and *Dylan Thomas and the Bohemians*, are illuminating on the subject of bohemianism. On the other hand, I find it difficult not to be considerably repelled by Caitlin Thomas. She grew up in a rackety bohemian household, but her brother John and her two sisters, Nicolette and Brigit, did not have the same deformations of personality as she did. She was by turns sullen, withdrawn, drunken, noisy, violent, bitter, envious and promiscuous. She believed, quite without merit, that she had a great talent (for dancing) and that this had been thwarted, largely by her husband.

In fact, as the photographs of her in the mid- and late-1930s—taken by her mother's lesbian lover—show, she had no talent at all. She is too plump to be a dancer and her poses, by a river bank in a translucent flowered dress, the kind of thing one might expect Victorian fairies to wear, are nothing other than ridiculous. She makes it clear in her book that the desire for dramatic effect always acted as a screen between her and honesty and sincerity. Alas, behind layers of superficiality often lie simply more layers of the same. In the photos of them together, and even of her on her own, there is something hard in her face, square-jawed, angry with life, even when she tries to look romantic.

Of course, Dylan Thomas was not a model husband, nor was he ever likely to be one (Caitlin would not have wanted him if he had been). A poem by Thomas's friend, Norman Cameron, an advertising executive and occasional poet who died in the same year as he, wrote a poem about Thomas called 'The Dirty Little Accuser' whose first stanza goes:[6]

Who invited him in? What was he doing here,
That insolent little ruffian, that crapulous lout?
When he quitted a sofa, he left behind him a smear.
My wife says he even tried to paw her about.

Near the beginning of *Double Drink Story*, Caitlin gives her side of the relationship: 'We belonged, no question about it, to the Greats, whose solemn duty was to surfeit ourselves limitlessly with drink, to wild extinction, only to begin again… Through degradation came purification. The lower we got, the higher we got… It was all part of that ridiculous romantic myth that said: not until you have passed through the Gates of Hell, not until you have passed through the blinding baptism of fire, are you fit to be a creator of the genuine burning stuff.'[7]

No doubt the American society-women who threw themselves at Thomas, who was none too clean and by no means physically attractive, probably thought they were serving some transcendent cleansing cause by doing so. And his frequently outrageous behaviour much resembled that of the Russian holy fools. It was evidence of his devotion to poetry, as the Russian holy fool's behaviour was evidence of his devotion to God. 'Never, I suppose, will it be settled how much his personality was the expression of faith, excitement, and rapture with its attendant ecstasies; how much was shrewd calculation and the sheer result of hankering after power; how much was unbridled lust.' Vogel-Jørgensen wrote this of Rasputin but it applies equally (almost) to Thomas:

One sees in her why the injunction to know thyself was deemed so important at the Temple of Apollo. The fact that Thomas obviously was capable of what Caitlin called 'the genuine burning stuff' was a problem for someone who craved attention for her own talent. She resented both

Dylan's waywardness and the increasing attention his genius received. In my youth and early adulthood I subscribed to the gates-of-hell theory, although I preferred to observe them rather than actually go through them. Dylan Thomas himself always returned to the petty-bourgeois comfort of his parental home after a few weeks sojourn through the gates.

When I am in Laugharne I visit the peaceful churchyard of St Martin's in which Thomas lies buried. It would be worth visiting even without its most famous resident. Among its yew and other trees it has the usual number (for this part of the world) of people drowned at sea at an early age. Thomas's simple tomb, a wooden cross painted white with black lettering, is very moving. He died aged thirty nine, killed in effect by the necessity he felt to take on the role of *poète maudit*. As he never fully matured as a man it is difficult even to imagine him in old age.

I ask myself unanswerable questions whenever I contemplate the simple cross of his grave. Was his art in fact inseparable from his life? If he had lived differently— that is to say, more sensibly—would he have achieved more and better? Or was, in fact, the chaos necessary to his production? Did his genius (evident very early in his life) excuse or mitigate the bad behaviour that so adversely affected the lives of his three children, none of whom fully escaped the effects of his selfish and insouciant parenting?

This question is compounded by the fact that Caitlin, who died more than fifty years after him, is now buried (at her own request) beside him, her name and dates painted in the same manner on the reverse of Thomas's cross—she who wrote so many disparaging things about him.

After his death, she lived most of her life in Italy where she took up with an Italian, Guiseppe Fazio, who had worked in the film industry. Unexpectedly she had, at the age of forty nine, a son by him—Francesco. I am not sure, if I had been either Guiseppe or Francesco, that I would have been altogether pleased by Caitlin's choice of last resting-place. I would have taken it to mean that her life subsequent to the death of Dylan had been but some kind of fill-in between his death and hers. Her first memoir, after all, had been titled *Leftover Life to Kill* (whose cover of the American edition has a picture of her in profile looking uncommonly like Mrs Thatcher).

There is something heart-rending about her reunion in the grave with Dylan, as if theirs had been a love story destroyed by immaturity, egotism and pig-headedness, but which was nevertheless the only event of her life. I warm slightly to Caitlin when I look at the inscription on the back of Dylan's white cross; and I think of the inscription I once saw over the gate of a cemetery in Guatemala: 'Through this gate all quarrels are forgotten, all sins forgiven.'

Nearby is another moving grave, with the simple inscription in stone, 'PAUL FREDERICK OEHLER, 1940-1987, POET, SCHOLAR FRIEND'. Oehler was an American academic who taught English literature at Sacramento City College and wrote *Dylan Thomas: A Bibliography of Criticism*, published in 1965, and 342 pages long. He was such a lover of Dylan Thomas that he travelled to Laugharne twelve times and was inclined to imitate his hero too closely in the matter of drinking. On his twelfth and final trip to

Laugharne, Oehler suffered a severe haemorrhage on the transatlantic flight and was rushed to hospital on arrival in England, where he died. In view of his retirement three years earlier and his heavy drinking, it seems to me likely that he suffered from cirrhosis of the liver and oesophageal varices, from which bleeding is often severe and frequently fatal.

Despite appearances to the contrary, he was not a bohemian according to the short memoir by his friend William Minor: 'I don't have many friends I would call "gentlemen"… but Paul Oehler was a gentleman, not of any corny old school but the genuine sort… carting an inherent dignity which—for all the damage he could do to himself, and he did considerable—I seldom saw him put aside for long. For all Paul's contemporaneity—his tattoos…—he was of some other world: archetypal, historical, transcendent… A paradox: a sensitive cerebral poet who collected stamps and recordings by Callas and lived with his mother in a turquoise Victorian home.'

On the other hand, the appropriation of Dylan Thomas by modern counter-culture is irritating. First, Dylan's bohemianism depended upon the contrast with respectability. Dylan had no such destructive ambitions of respectability. Second, Dylan was in many ways a tradition-alist. He was religious, at least in a broad sense, and, though he was a dropout from school, he was extremely well-versed in English literature and would not in the least have sympathised with the jettisoning of literary tradition. He never set himself up as if trying to found a political party; and his poetry concerned itself largely with the transcendent questions of human life: growth and decay, our response to nature, the effect of time and the approach of death.

1   She was the wife of the famous historian, A.J.P. Taylor, who detested Dylan as a sponger, a thief and a liar. He was all of those things, it is true, and yet.

2   This is not as far-fetched as it sounds—nothing is these days. In France they managed pictoriographically to remove Albert Camus's cigarette, as if it had been a member of the Soviet Politburo fallen into disfavour. Satire is dangerous nowadays not because of the censorship rules of tyrannical government, but because it is prophecy, or even prediction.

3   Also the author of one of the chapters in *The God that Failed*, edited by Richard Crossman, a collection of essays recounting six famous authors' disillusionment with communism. Their illusionment in the first place was the more interesting phenomenon.

4   It was in a love poem, and it seemed to me to carry quite a burden of pain in it.

5   His friend and fellow-Swansea poet, Vernon Watkins, was a bank clerk.

6   If this is what your friends write about you, what about your enemies? My copy on Norman Collins's collected poems, incidentally, which I bought second-hand, has the strong smell of tobacco smoke about it.

7   'Perhaps the most prominent feature of holy fools was their addiction to extremes of behaviour. Moderation was not a virtue they pursued. In fact, in the value system which they represented, moderation was not a virtue but a vice. Sinning in an ostentatious way and then doing penance in a similarly ostentatious way… was what [holy fools] practised.' Ewa M. Thompson, *op. cit.* p 14.

26

Hellfire

It was time to return to Bridgnorth. How well we know and love the road, though its meaning has changed for us from the happy time when we drove it twice a week for my wife's work. In the words of Houseman:

The happy highways where I went
And cannot come again.

Next door but two to our house in Bridgnorth is a little white cottage with the following words painted in black on its front:

In this house
Lived the learned and eloquent
Richard Baxter
1640-41

For some reason I misread for a number of years the word 'eloquent' as 'elegant'. It was an odd mistake as Baxter, a famous divine in his time and author of some two hundred pietistic works, believed that a baby who died before baptism was destined for eternal hellfire. He didn't much approve of Bridgnorth because it was a royalist town and he was a puritan, so he moved to and preached instead in Kidderminster where he felt more at home.